Building a Book, Binding a Poem

Artists' Books in the Classroom

Meg Kennedy
Liz Abrams-Morley

Building a Book, Binding a Poem

Published by

Book Arts Press

P. O. Box 199
Wynnewood, PA 19096-3810
www.book-arts-press.com

Design by Jon A. Pastor
Cover Design by Jon A. Pastor

Library of Congress Cataloging in Publication Data

Library of Congress Control Number: 2009913338

Kennedy, Meg
Abrams-Morley, Liz.
Building a Book, Binding a Poem / Meg Kennedy & Liz Abrams-Morley

ISBN 978-0-9795861-0-1

Edition 1.0.0

TABLE OF CONTENTS

Chapter 1 – Why Books? Why Poetry? 1
- What do we mean by Poetry? 1
- What are Artists' Books? 2
- Why Write Poetry? 3
- Why Make Books? 3

Chapter 2 – A Time Line of Book History 5

Chapter 3 – Let's Begin: Making Choices 13

Chapter 4 – Creating Visual Environments 17
- Crayon Resist 19
- Embossing 20
- Frottage (Texture Rubbing) 21
- Stencils 22
- Spatter and Sponge Painting 24
- Spray Paint "Tie Dye" 26
- Paper Weaving, Piercing, & Sewing 28
- Bubble Marbling 31
- Chalk Marbling 32
- Suminagashi Marbling 34
- Paste Papers 36
- Nature Printing 38
- Watercolor Washes with Alterations 41
- Final Note 44

Chapter 5 – Creating Poetry-Friendly Environments 45
- A Word About Warming Up 48
- Some Warm Up Activities 49
  - Journaling 49
  - Free Writing 50
  - Word Bowls 50
  - Writing from Photos or Postcards 51
  - Using The Other Senses 51
  - Use of Music and Movement 51
  - Making Lists 52
  - Observation: My Mother's Tray Game 52
- A Word About the Power of Limits 53

Chapter 6 – Book-Making 101: Just the Basics 55
Materials & Tools 55
A Few Basic Techniques 60
Accordion Book 63
Pamphlet 65
Stab-Bound Book 71
Chapter 7 – Revision and Evaluation 77
Revision: The Art of Seeing All Over Again 77
A Word About Revision and the Artist Book 81
Evaluation of Student Work 82
Chapter 8 – Getting Words onto the Page 85
Hand Lettering 86
Computer Type 88
Rubber Stamp Letters 88
Stencils 89
Ransom Note Collage 89
Masking 90
Emboss 91
Chapter 9 – Artist Book Projects 93
Preface 93
Project #1: Environmental Album 94
Project #2: Unfolding Memories 97
Project #3: "It was a dark and stormy night..." 100
Project #4: He Said/She Said 106
Writing Prompts for Projects 4 and 5 109
Project #5: French Door Dialogue 111
Project #6: "P.O.V." 114
Project #7: Thematic Flag Book 119
Project #8: "Mapping a Life" 123
Project #9: A Collaborative Album 128
Project #10: Foreign Correspondence 132
Project #11: Altered Books & Found Poetry 138
Project #12: Free-Form Exploration 144
Chapter 10 – Appendix & Templates 149
Chapter 11 – Resources 163
Chapter 12 – Bibliography 167
Chapter 13 – Acknowledgements 169

1 Why Books? Why Poetry?

We come together as two artists: each involved with creating books, each with a separate primary interest as well as areas of overlapping interest. Liz is a poet; Meg is a book artist. As colleagues and collaborators, we have found parallels in the ways we select and revise as we work in our individual art forms. In working together, we look for ways in which the marriage of form and content combine into a new creation, another level of communication. In *Building a Book, Binding a Poem*, we introduce you and your students to the process of expressing yourselves in word, image, and book form. Our projects are designed with fifth through twelfth graders in mind, but can be adapted for use by younger students or by adults. Poetry—the distillation of image and feeling into words—and artists' books—volumes created as individual works of art—both express the uniqueness of the creator, the multitude of possibilities, and the universal appeal of art forms that date back to the dawn of civilization.

> *Poetry is an inclusive term. . . a thought, an idea, a story, a memory, a feeling set into a design of words.*

What do we mean by Poetry?

Many of us were taught that writing poetry requires mastering certain elements of form, preset patterns of rhyme or meter. When students are confronted with instruction to "write a poem," they will offer up an immediate objection: *But I can never think of rhyming words or get the right number of syllables on a line.* We encourage you to consider a broader, looser definition of poetry than words that rhyme or fit a given pattern. In many languages other than English, poetry has always been composed in free verse, without end rhymes or set meter; in English, the predominance of end rhyme faded when Walt Whitman introduced us to his *Leaves of Grass* in 1855.

If a poem is not a series of lines that rhyme, what is it? A poem is a compact piece of writing that contains one or more poetic elements (rhythm, figurative language, condensed use of language). When a student compares the sound of popcorn popping to the sound of rain on a tin roof, that's poetry. When another describes a day at the beach by identifying the odd mixture of scents—salt spray, coconut oil and pizza—that's poetry. For the purposes of this book, *expressive writing* or *intense language* may be considered synonyms for poetry. Poetry is an inclusive term: think of it as a thought, an idea, a story, a memory, a feeling set into a design of words.[1]

What are Artists' Books?

Although entire books have been written about the subject, for our purposes, artists' books are personally expressive, limited edition books that use the structure, visual elements, and text to communicate their message. Essentially, it's a book that is a piece of art, a sequence of visual spaces that creates a whole beyond its parts, a new way of seeing that is built on multiple images and texts.[2] Employing the same media as "wall art," e.g. paint, collage, photography, printing, etc., artists' books marry form and content, the visual and the verbal, so that every detail of the book structure articulates the idea or theme of the text. A simple example of this would be using handmade paper that includes

Artists' books marry form and content, the visual and the verbal, so that every detail of the book structure articulates the idea or theme of the text.

[1] Nancy Cecil, *For the Love of Language*
[2] Richard Minsky, Director of the Center for Book Arts in NYC

seeds, leaves, or petals for a book about growing. Artists' books recognize the interaction that is inherent between a book and its reader: by opening and closing a book, by turning pages forward and backward, the reader or viewer engages with the artwork more intimately than when it's hung on the wall.

Why Write Poetry?

The ability to write poetry (as we have defined it here) is not dependent on a student's age or academic accomplishments. The raw materials of a poem include the poet's feelings, history, and perception, so every human being has the background necessary to craft poetic writing. Poetry allows writers to connect their five senses with their feelings and their feelings with thoughts.

The students we have taught, from kindergartners to senior citizens, show us that they enjoy making these connections; they enjoy making their connections into poems. They work with enthusiasm. They make happy noise. This is an activity that taps both reason and feeling, that simultaneously calls on the scientific principals of observation of our universe and on the free play of imagination, that allows all sorts of learners and all levels of achievers to experience a "success." The educational advantages of such an activity are legion.

Why Make Books?

As seemingly commonplace as books are, a book of one's own never fails to impress even the most disinterested student. Each handmade book represents choices made, skills achieved, and personal expression acknowledged. Writing, designing, and assembling a collection of pages into a binding makes each student feel that his work is important and permanent.

In a society that is becoming increasingly removed from physical process, making books with readily available materials (paper, cardboard, thread, glue, etc.) restores one's confidence in the ability to construct rather than just buy a ready-made commodity. Many teachers have observed that non-traditional

Poetry writing can:

- make students feel creative, competent, happy
- make students more open to and interested in understanding the writing of others (so they want to read)
- make students want to master skills that will help them to write (to improve spelling and even grammar)
- help students understand their own feelings
- help students explore and understand the feelings of others, walk in another's shoes, metaphorically speaking
- enhance students' curiosity and perception; once aroused, this enhanced curiosity can spill over into interest in other areas of learning
- reach the non-traditional learner since poetry enters the listener's understanding mind through the heart more often than it does through the head
- help students express themselves better in writing as well as in public speaking
- encourage thinking which is non-linear
- increase the power of students' imaginations

Making books can:

- encourage writing, which nourishes reading skills
- encourage students to express personal statements, structure narratives, and collect information
- help students to compile and organize information and ideas thematically
- demystify commercially made books, thereby making them more accessible (and desirable)
- concretely show how to follow logical steps to a well-defined goal
- help students to sequence information into a narrative
- help students to learn about selection and revision when dealing with the limitations of a book's format (e.g. number of pages or size of the book)
- offer opportunities to explore design, imagery, illustration, thematic development, and the use of various art materials
- foster an awareness of how one of the more influential cultural developments evolved in various civilizations

learners often can express themselves more easily in an assignment that involves manual as well as intellectual abilities.

Besides all this, bookmaking is *fun*: it allows middle school and high school students (as well as adults) to learn in the kindergarten "chaos" of play with glue, paint, paper, scissors, and string. And what better way to sneak in lessons about grammar or measuring or sequencing information than in the midst of a project in which each student is personally invested?

As a Balinese proverb states, "We have no art, we do everything as well as possible"; so bookmaking demystifies and makes accessible an art form in which everyone can participate. For these and numerous other literacy, organizational, aesthetic, and cultural reasons, we believe in the value of incorporating book arts with other teaching strategies.

2 A Time Line of Book History

A real history of book making would be several times longer than this volume, but we're including a time line of highlights that occurred over the course of 5,500 years so that teachers can make students aware of the legacy of books throughout history, diverse cultures and geographical areas. All cultures made books for the same reason: to collect, preserve, and communicate information and ideas. At first using available natural materials—clay, stone, wood, bark, bamboo, leaves—and later creating materials on which to write—papyrus, cloth, leather, parchment, paper—early civilizations developed book formats that arose from the materials at hand.

A shorthand evolution of the modern book form has three steps: the scroll, the accordion book, and the codex. Elaborating on these steps, and ignoring the many idiosyncratic forms found throughout history, we have the following evolutions:

- The first "real" books were scrolls, which is where the word "volume" comes from: scrolls were rolled and the Latin term for roll is *volumen*.
- Some scrolls were eventually folded, in smaller segments, back and forth like a fan-fold. This is the accordion or concertina form. It wasn't used everywhere scrolls appeared: some materials, such as papyrus, couldn't be easily folded (without cracking at the fold), but others, such as parchment, stiffened silk and linen, and especially paper, adapted to this new form which was more compact and flat for storage.

- In some parts of the world—chiefly east Asia—accordion books were sewn through one side to create a book with front and back covers and writing on both sides of the (folded) page. In other parts of the world, hinged boards covered inside with dark wax were used as notebooks—again providing a "volume" with front and back covers and "pages" inside. Later, individual sheets of parchment and paper were folded and sewn to create a spine to which covers were attached. These forms all had in common covers, pages, and a connecting spine: the codex.

The rest of the evolution of book making mainly involves developments in human communication, artistic design, technological advances, and the use of materials. The time line gives an overview of how the various forms developed out of one another, where they fit historically and geographically in the world.

Since our goal is to help teachers incorporate book arts into their curricula, we're hoping that this rapid romp through five millennia provides some prompts. Here are a few ideas:

- A social studies class could use Asian book forms in a unit on that region.
- The various materials (e.g. clay, bark, wood, leaves, fabric, paper, etc.) that were used for writing in various cultures could be linked to environmental studies, and how natural resources affect cultural development.
- The creation of papyrus as a writing material takes into account plant parts and properties; a bookish science lesson. Making paper is another one.

- Multicultural studies could include Egyptian myths on papyrus scrolls, haikus on rice paper or silk, South American folktales on bark, Native American history on leather.
- History and/or Art classes on Medieval and Renaissance periods could investigate the writing, illuminated decoration, and gilding that was used in manuscripts.

Let your imagination wander freely!

BCE (BC)

3500 | 3000 | 2500 | 2000 | 1500 | 1000 | 500

3500
- Sumerian pictograms on stone & clay

3500
- Chinese pictograms on bamboo, wood, & clay

3000
- Cuneiform in Mesopotamia on clay tablets

3000-2500
- Indian writing on stone, copper, wood, & palm leaves
- Egyptian hieroglyphs on stone, wood, palm leaves, linen, & papyrus scrolls

2000
- Chinese writing system invented— on bark, wood, & silk scrolls

1500
- Syrian cuneiform developed using only 22 signs (first alphabetic writing)

1200
- Phoenicians use non-cuneiform alphabet (22 letters)

1000-700
- Greek alphabet, 24 letters, on wax tablets of slate
- Aramaic writing (later evolved into Hebrew and Arabic)

600
- Greeks & Etruscans in Italy develop Roman alphabet

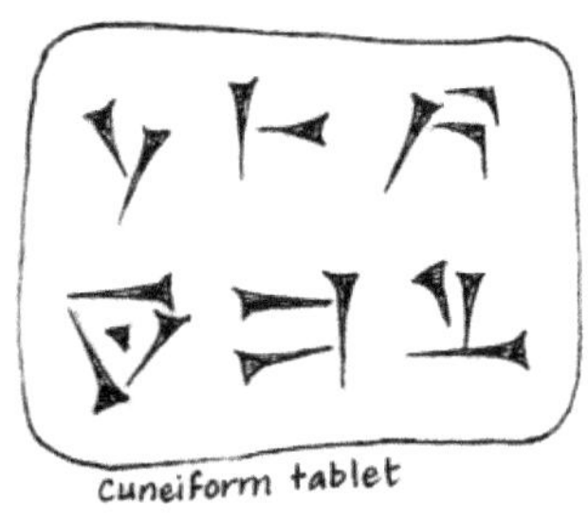
Cuneiform tablet

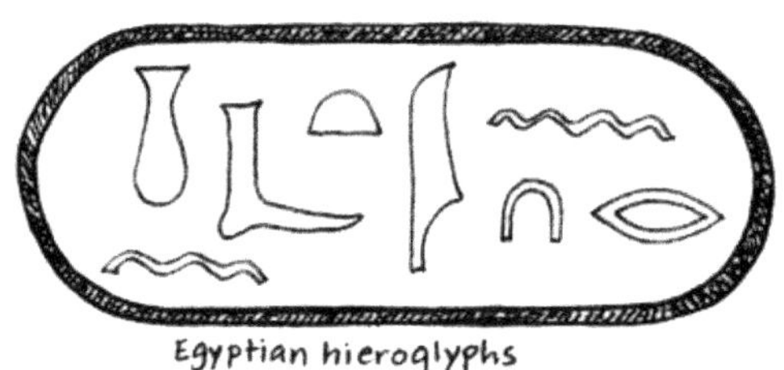
Egyptian hieroglyphs

BCE (BC) | **CE (AD)**

500 | 300 | 100 | 0 | 100 | 300 | 500 | 700

400
- Latins conquer Etruscans, adopt Roman alphabet

300
- Romans inscribe alphabet on stone monuments, write on papyrus, linen scrolls, wax tablets of wood (codex)

200
- Wooden and bamboo slat accordions joined with cords used throughout Asia

200
- Parchment used in place of papyrus

100
- Chinese invent paper

300
- Romans spread Latin language and alphabet throughout their empire

600
- Oldest continuous newspaper published monthly in Peking, China using woodblocks

600-900
- Earliest paper accordion books (folded scrolls) found in China

700
- Emperor Charlemagne promotes the writing of books throughout the Holy Roman Empire
- Papermaking introduced to the West

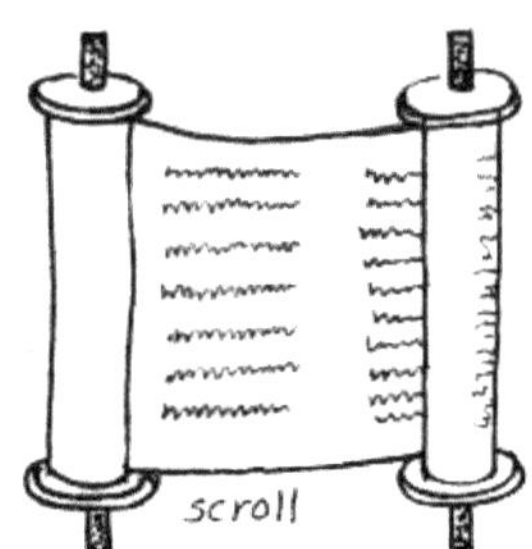

scroll

wax tablet codex

CE (AD)

800-1000
- Scriptoria established in monasteries throughout Europe
- Illuminated manuscripts
- Cyrillic alphabet (from Greek) develops further east

1100:
- Chinese invent movable type characters (first clay, later wood)
- Rise of secular books and scribes in guilds and workshops
- Books available to the middle class for the first time

1200-1300
- Rise of universities in Europe, books in greater demand

1390
- First book printed with movable metal letters in China

1440
- Johann Gutenberg invents the movable type printing press

1450
- The Gutenberg Bible

1476
- William Caxton sets up first English printing press

CE (AD)

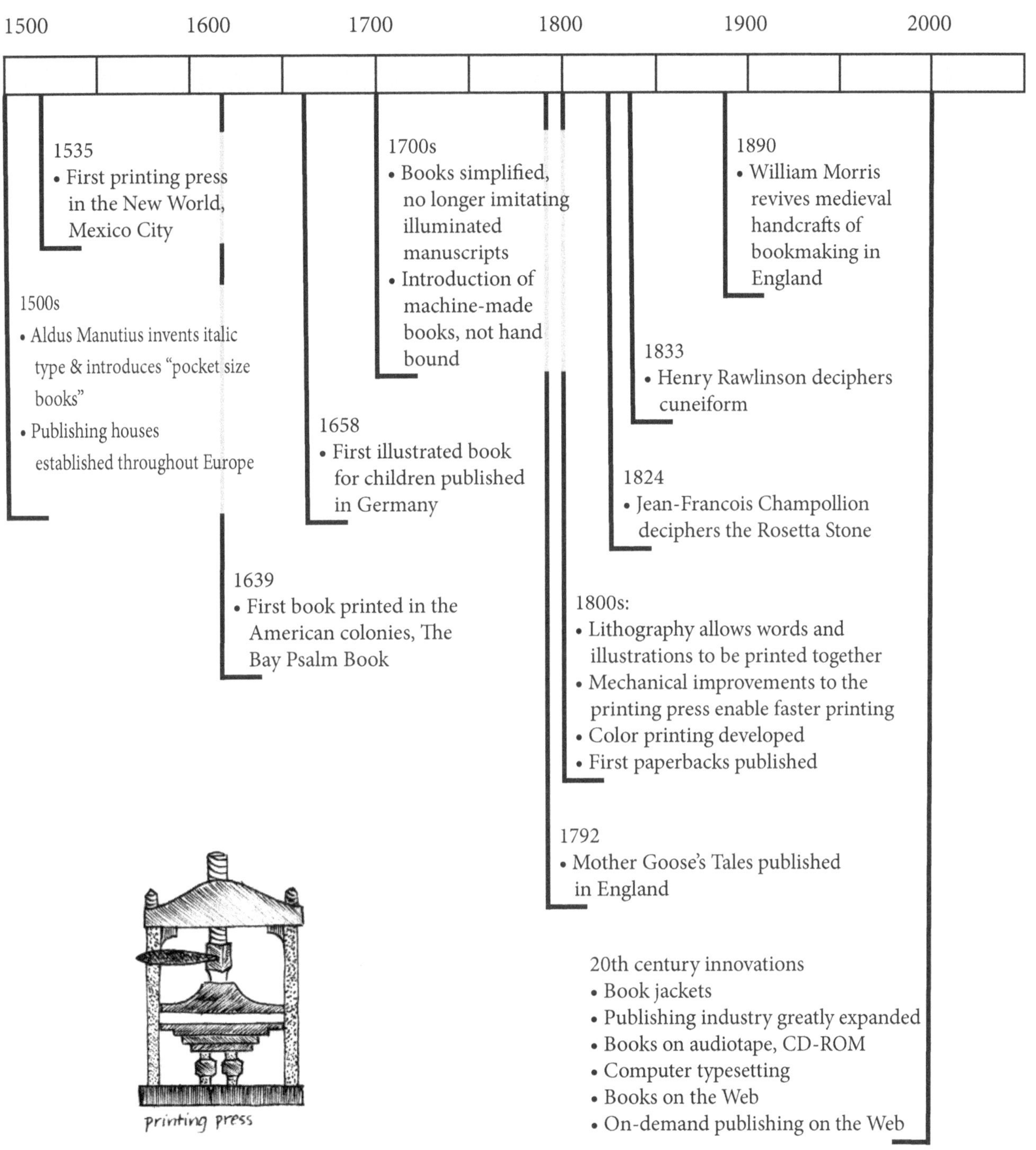

1500
1600
1700
1800
1900
2000
1535
• First printing press in the New World, Mexico City
1500s
• Aldus Manutius invents italic type & introduces "pocket size books"
• Publishing houses established throughout Europe
1639
• First book printed in the American colonies, The Bay Psalm Book
1658
• First illustrated book for children published in Germany
1700s
• Books simplified, no longer imitating illuminated manuscripts
• Introduction of machine-made books, not hand bound
1792
• Mother Goose's Tales published in England
1800s:
• Lithography allows words and illustrations to be printed together
• Mechanical improvements to the printing press enable faster printing
• Color printing developed
• First paperbacks published
1824
• Jean-Francois Champollion deciphers the Rosetta Stone
1833
• Henry Rawlinson deciphers cuneiform
1890
• William Morris revives medieval handcrafts of bookmaking in England
20th century innovations
• Book jackets
• Publishing industry greatly expanded
• Books on audiotape, CD-ROM
• Computer typesetting
• Books on the Web
• On-demand publishing on the Web
printing press

3 Let's Begin: Making Choices

Everyone has something to say and most people like to play with colors, designs, and textures. *Building a Book, Binding a Poem* combines these creative impulses and gives students a place to play with words, images, ideas, paper, and a variety of art materials. You don't need to be a poet or a book artist to guide your students through these projects and explore the connections between text and form. The book includes writing prompts, clear directions for making a variety of book forms, and ways to integrate these projects into other areas of the curriculum. Although we focus on students in grades 5–12, some of the projects and exercises suggest alternatives for younger or older audiences.

You don't need to be a poet or a book artist to guide your students through these projects and explore the connections between text and form.

Throughout our program, we emphasize the importance of self-expression, the practice of revision, and the joy of process—not just the goal of product. We believe that engaging students in an exploration of books and writing from new perspectives encourages and reinforces literacy and creative thinking.

Making Choices

Artistic communication is all about making choices. Choosing words, materials, colors, sounds, textures, images, movement, and form defines the artist's voice and invites the audience to communicate with the work. When we began to collaborate, we discovered that our criteria for selecting or rejecting various elements in our work overlapped in many ways. For each individual piece, certain options need to be considered, such as audience, mood, appearance, length or size, and time constraints. We find that a good way to proceed is to generate questions about these numerous choices. The following list will help you and your students envision a project.

Artistic communication is all about making choices.

What will this book be about?

- What will be its subject or theme?
- Will you try to evoke a mood or emotion?

What is the audience for this book?

- Is it a personal statement that I'm willing to share?
- Is it an intimate communication to a member of my family?
- Is it a public statement?
- Is it a children's book?
- Is it a book for other artists?
- Is it an informational book for a specific audience? (e.g. musicians, birdwatchers, soccer fans, etc.)

Which senses will I try to appeal to?

- Will this be primarily a visual book?
- Should there be textures to be touched?
- How could smells be included? (scratch 'n' sniff?)
- Is there anything to hear in a book?
- How could I include taste?

How will I engage the reader or viewer?

- Will the book have movable parts? secret compartments? pop-ups? pockets that hold messages?

- Should I use transparent sheets of plastic or acetate for windows that reveal? reflective mylar or actual mirrors to reflect the reader? opaque sheets to conceal what comes next?
- Should the book be tied shut with a ribbon? Can it be latched in some way that requires the reader to act?
- Can the size or shape of a book attract or repel the audience? (e.g. How do you, as a reader, react to a book that fits in the palm of your hand vs. a large leather-bound volume in a case?)
- What will I show or tell and what will I leave a mystery?

Will I start with words (text) or forms (bookbinding styles) or colors (a red book) or materials (special papers, fabrics, metals, etc.)?

- If I start with text, will I use only my own words, or add another writer's text(s)? Does further research need to be done?
- How does a bookbinding style suggest a theme for a book? (e.g., a scroll creates a different environment than a pop-up book.)
- What non-verbal messages can be communicated through color or texture?
- How can I create the appropriate environment or mood without specific images or words?

What physical limitations do I want or need to set for this project?

- Is there a deadline?
- What is my budget? (cost of materials)
- What techniques do I know or can I learn?
- What is the length of the text and how will it affect the size of the book?
- How many copies do I need to make?
- If I want multiple copies, will I make each by hand or rely on technology (e.g. a photocopying machine)?

How will the physical appearance support or express the theme of the book?

- Will I use a horizontal or vertical format? (e.g. a tall skinny book probably would not suggest the desert or the ocean.)
- Would other shapes help to convey my theme? Consider a round, heart-shaped, square, or triangular format.
- Will I use color, texture, shape, imagery, or words to present the title? (e.g. A book about winter would probably not be yellow, orange, bright green, etc.)

What other design choices do I need to consider?

- Should I follow the pattern of a fixed writing form (e.g. sonnet, haiku) or a free form of my own making?
- Is there one type of binding that is exactly appropriate or should I combine forms?
- Will I illustrate the text or suggest imagery abstractly? *
- How will white space (space on the page without text) be used?
- Should I use conventions of writing (e.g. capitalization, punctuation, paragraphing)? If not, why not?
- Should every page be the same size and shape? Many book forms can accommodate pages of different sizes as well as fold-outs or extensions to pages.
- Should the cover be soft and pliable or hard and protective?
- Should I limit the palette of colors used?
- How will I create order in the book? (e.g. Will I divide the text into sections, create physical divisions with the binding, include an epilogue or epigraph?)

These lists suggest many of the choices you as an artist might want to consider in making your artists' books. Keep in mind that choices are good, but that boundaries are important as well. Set some parameters. Start by making a few key decisions about your book. This will allow your project to move out of the thinking stage and into form.

In creating their own artists' books, your students will:

- explore handmade books and poetic texts
- investigate the artistic choices that define these works
- practice poetic observation and make creative journals
- build poems from such familiar categories as lists, monologues, and directions
- choose from several book forms to see how form can influence content
- learn about the historic origins of different book forms
- experience poetry as an accessible and personal art form
- be encouraged to write and to collect their writings in books of their own
- employ critical thinking skills
- experience the freedom and responsibility of making creative choices

* While some artists' books are illustrated, just as often their "pictures" are abstract or symbolic, suggested through color, media, size, repetition, or placement on a page. The following chapter, "Creating Visual Environments," will further explore some methods of providing imagery without actually drawing.

4 Creating Visual Environments

Book artists often face the visual equivalent of writer's block: fear of white space. That endless expanse (even if it's only 9×12") of pure, perfect white, of nothingness, seems to taunt and intimidate the visual artist, who needs only to apply a mark to the page to "break the ice." But where? What kind of a mark? What color/shape/size? What tool and media to use? So, I make a mark, and then what?

A good way to plow through this labyrinth is to generate a variety of environments on paper. You can use numerous techniques to "resurface" your plain paper into subtle backgrounds for words or images, graphic designs that frame or accent, and textures that add dimension. This section introduces numerous paper-surfacing methods that can stage, inspire, suggest, echo, or illustrate writing. Some papers are even interesting enough to stand on their own. Our purpose with these activities, however, is not to produce pieces of finished artwork, but to create environments that invite the artist and the audience to become involved with the page.

Create environments which invite the artist and the audience to become involved with the page

By changing the color and texture of your paper; by adding layers and attachments; by piercing, tearing, cutting, joining, and interweaving pieces of paper, a two-dimensional page can take on a sculptural aspect. These alterations can capture and focus attention on a page, break the expected routine of words on pages, and conceal or reveal information. Visually interesting pages are a hallmark of artists' books and all of this can be achieved without knowing how to draw!*

The various paper-surfacing techniques use easily available equipment and materials. None requires a large budget. Some, however, are messy and need space and time for drying as well as room ventilation. All can be done in the classroom, and if you have a sink, it will be even easier. Most methods can stand alone, but combining two or more techniques makes a richer environment to which to respond.

* A common complaint among students is "I can't draw." These techniques can silence that whine.

Crayon Resist

Similar to batik fabric designs, crayon resist on paper can produce bold graphic spaces in which to stage writing. The environment created will depend on the colors chosen and the marks made. Random, rhythmic crayon marks that go off the page are usually better in terms of design than intentional images or words written in crayon and placed in the middle of the page.

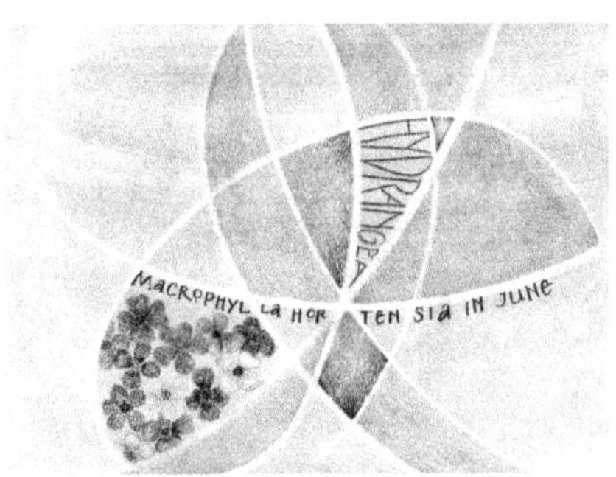

Directions:

1. Draw or write with a white crayon on white paper. Random marks yield surprisingly nice results.
2. Paint the entire page with a diluted ink mixture. *[Hint: put scrap paper down on the work table so that brushstrokes can extend off the sheet without undue mess.]*
3. The crayon lines will resist the colored ink and define areas in which to plan a design or composition.
4. Once the paper is dry, you can darken or accentuate certain areas with colored pencil or another color ink or paint.
5. If the paper curls, lightly spray the reverse side with water and either iron flat or press flat under a weight

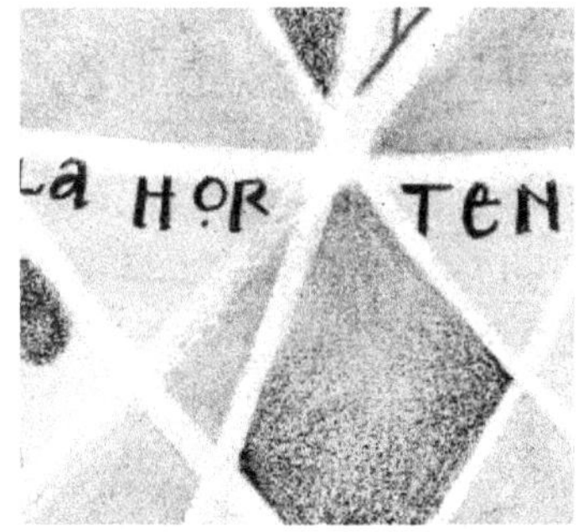

Materials: :

- white crayons
- medium- to heavy-weight drawing paper
- a dilute mixture of water soluble ink in water (several drops of ink in a half cup of water) or diluted watercolor (which will not be as intense)
- 1″ paint brush for each color
- optional: colored pencils

Embossing

Embossing (a shape emerging above the surface of the paper) can act like a subtle suggestion or echo for the text. Embossing stencils should be kept very clean and not used for the stencil projects on page 22. If commercial stencils are used, get ones that are colored plastic so that they will show through your paper. A less expensive alternative is to cut shapes (or letters or images) from cover weight paper or poster board. If cut out carefully, you'll have both a positive and a negative stencil to use.

Materials:

- commercial or "homemade" stencils (cut from oaktag or cardstock)

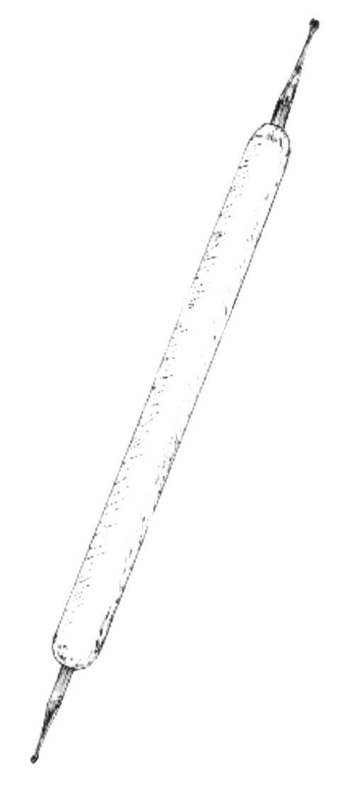

- medium-weight paper
- ball-point embossing tools or blunted bamboo skewers or "dead" ballpoint pens (no ink)
- light box or easily accessible light source (e.g. window)

Directions:

1. Position a stencil beneath a sheet of paper; you may want to lightly tape it into place. Hold the paper up against a window so that light shows through and reveals the shape beneath or place the paper on a light box.
2. With a stick or stylus, trace the design cut in the stencil through the paper. The shape will stick through the back of the paper.
3. If the paper is turned over and the stencil repositioned beneath the sheet, when you trace the design it will emerge in the opposite direction of the one you did in #2. When the image sticks up, it is embossed. When it's recessed, it's debossed.
4. Alternating embossing and debossing within a design adds interest.

A stencil cut from cardstock, sitting on a light box.

With a ball-point embossing tool, trace the pattern of the stencil through the paper.

Alternating embossing and debossing within a design.

Frottage (Texture Rubbing)

Rubbings from textured surfaces add design, dimension, and depth to a sheet. Since you will probably want to write over the image from the texture, lightly stroke the paper with graphite or colored pencils. Whatever media you choose needs to be dry. Crayons may be too waxy to write over. Pastel or charcoal will smear unless you seal them with a workable fixative spray.

Materials:
- textured surfaces (e.g. sandpaper, window screen, burlap, lace, cement, corduroy, corrugated cardboard, etc.)
- paper (light-weight, e.g. 20 lb. bond)
- colored pencils or graphite

Directions:

1. Lay paper over a textured surface.
2. With the side of a pencil, rub or color the paper to reveal the texture beneath.
3. Rub lightly for a background texture or more firmly for a prominent texture design.
4. Tips:
   - You can make one textured sheet and photocopy it to make duplicate backgrounds.
   - With colored pencil, you can emphasize portions of the textured background, especially if it contains recognizable images (e.g. leaves, squares).
   - Rub over texture in different directions to vary pattern.
   - Combine several textures on a sheet for more depth.
   - If graphite is used, one way to introduce a word is to "write" it with an eraser (removing the graphite).
   - Texture can be confined to a particular shape, e.g. a heart, by placing a stencil shape over the sheet of paper that is positioned over the texture. Rub over the texture within the shape of the stencil.

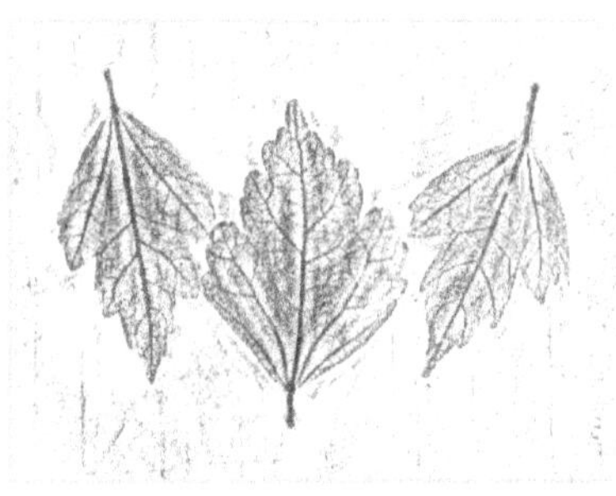

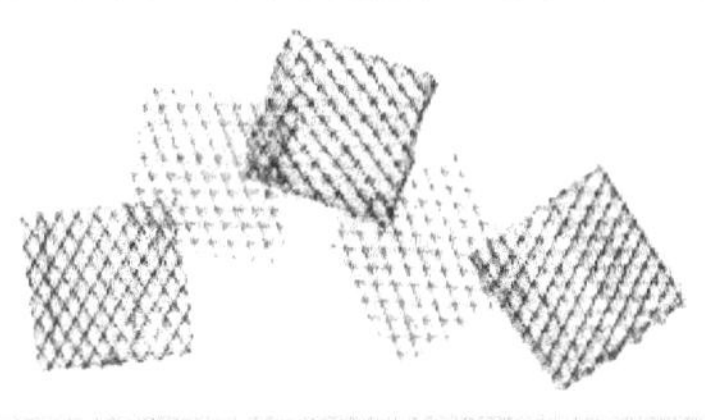

Stencils

Stenciling (coloring within or around a shape) is familiar as a decorative device on walls, etc., but used in book arts, it provides subtle backgrounds. Commercial stencils are commonly found in craft stores and can be used for this purpose. For a less pre-packaged, more individual look, however, stencils can be hand cut from acetate, mylar, or cardstock. Since the coloring media for stenciling is usually wet, you'll need clear Con-Tact® paper to cover the cardstock shapes you cut.* Hearts, flowers, leaves, and butterfly shapes are pretty but obvious; don't discount the subtle persuasiveness that abstract or rhythmic shapes can suggest as thematic backgrounds.

Materials:

- stencils, commercial or "homemade"
- paper (medium drawing weight)
- pastels & Q-tips®
- oil pastels & cotton balls
- stamp pad and sponge
- watercolor pan paints (e.g. cheap kids' set with 6-8 colors)

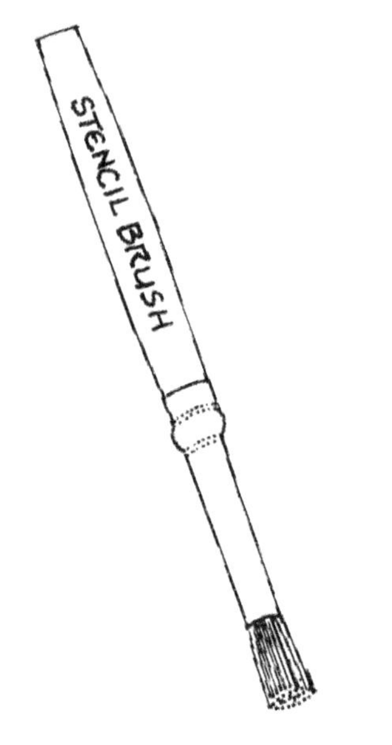

- stencil brushes
- colored pencils

Directions:

1. Position the stencil on the sheet of paper.
2. Designs can be transferred onto the page in several ways:
   - damp sponge or stencil brush and watercolor pans: Dab, stipple, or rub color away from the stencil onto the paper.
   - stamp pad and sponge: Dab or rub ink from edge of stencil onto the paper. You can leave the texture left by the sponge imprint or smooth it out.
   - colored pencil: Light "feather" strokes of the pencil from the stencil to the interior of the shape, solid coloring, or cross-hatching within stencil shape give a more definite image.
   - oil pastel: Color around the outside of the stencil shape with oil crayon and rub the color from the stencil onto the paper with a cotton ball for an airbrush effect.

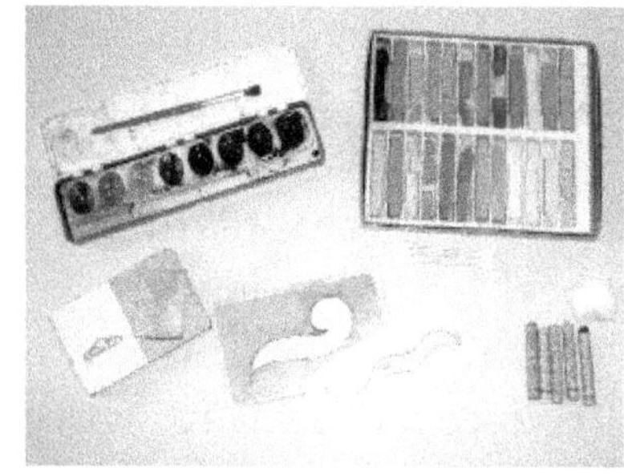

Stencil materials: paints & stencil brush; oil pastels & cotton ball; chalk pastels & Q-tips®; stamp pad & sponge; and homemade stencils

* Stencils can be made by cutting out a shape from a piece of cardstock, covering the shape on both sides with clear Con-Tact® paper, and cutting the Con-Tact® to conform to the shape of the stencil. Now the shape you want to use is waterproof.

- colored chalk or pastel: Rub Q-tip® on pastel, then stroke the colored Q-tip® away from the stencil edge onto the paper to make gradient color similar to old-fashioned theorem painting on cloth.

3. *Tips*:
   - Remember to overlap patterns for a more interesting background.
   - For a less static design, allow some shapes to run off the page.
   - When using chalk or pastel, lightly coat the stencilled page with a workable spray fixative to prevent smearing (spraying requires ventilation).
   - Combine on a page several of the stencil treatments to add intensity and depth.

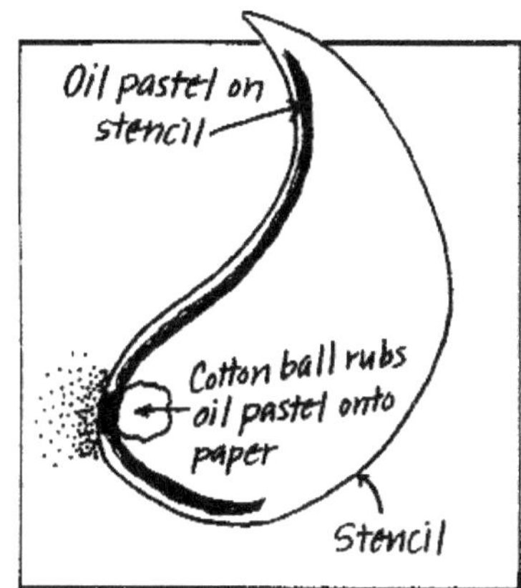

Using oil pastels with stencils gives an airbrush look.

Stencil (Sushi Grass) using oil pastel rubbed off stencil and overlapped

Spatter and Sponge Painting

Possibly the easiest of the techniques, these involve dabbing color onto paper with sponges of various textures and spraying dots of color onto paper with a toothbrush and stick. A cut stencil or torn sheet of paper can be laid across the page to mask out certain areas. Since the paint is only moistened (by misting it with water from a spray bottle), the color dries quickly and layers of color can be added.

Materials:

- various sponges—natural, manufactured, grainy, smooth (e.g. cosmetic sponge, car wash sponge, nylon scrub sponge for dishes, natural sea sponge)
- old toothbrush & stick (e.g. bamboo skewer, large toothpick, coffee stirrer)
- watercolor pan paints (e.g. cheap kids' set with 6-8 colors)
- spray bottle (fine spray) for water
- medium-weight paper
- 3-sided box for containing spatters

Directions:

1. Spatter painting should be done in a 3-sided box so that you don't spatter everything in the vicinity.
2. Stroke the dampened (not wet) cake of watercolor with the clean, dry toothbrush. Over the paper you want to decorate, hold the toothbrush with the bristles pointing down and stroke the bristles with the stick. *Make sure you bring the stick towards you or you'll speckle yourself instead of the paper.*

Starry sky spatter painting

3. *Tips*: this technique can be added over others, e.g. to add highlights to a sheet that has been bubble marbled, batiked, embossed, or paste papered. Use gold or silver paint over black or navy blue paper for a wonderful starry night.

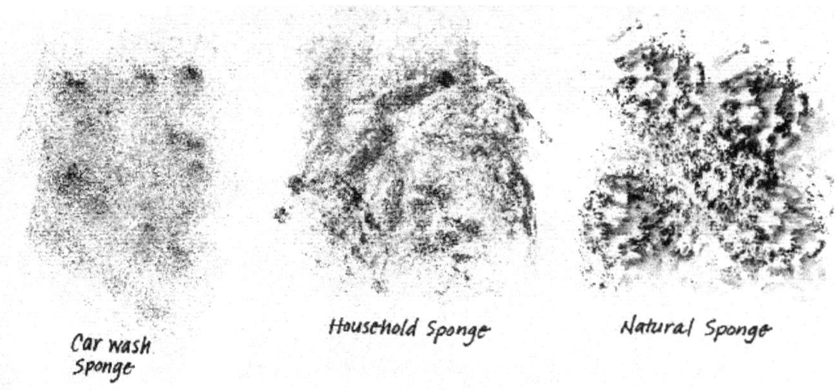

4. SPONGING is very immediate: dab a dry sponge onto damp paint or a stamp pad and then dab colored sponge onto paper.
5. Use different sponges to get various textures.
6. Sponge the entire sheet or mask off certain areas with stencils.

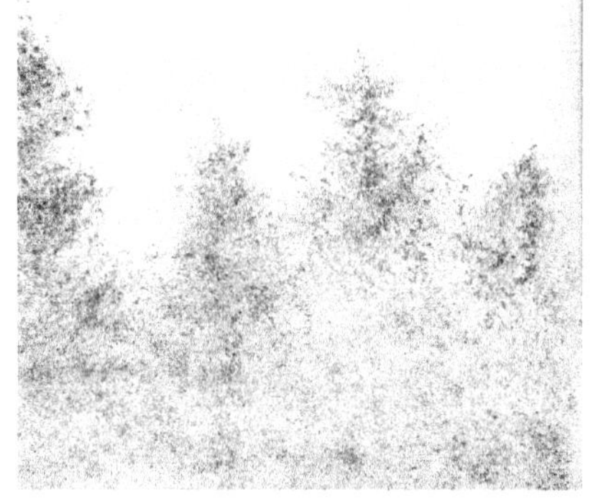

Sponged foliage

7. *Tip*: This technique can be overdone quite easily, so a light hand and a pale color are a good way to start.

Spray Paint "Tie Dye"

This technique produces a topographic quality to the paper, but requires sufficient ventilation since spray paint is used. The all-over design produced might be too much for a page with text, but can be useful as decorative paper for covering boards, or in collage.

Materials:

- medium- or light-weight drawing paper
- spray paint
- 3-sided box or drop cloth
- iron

Directions:

1. Take a sheet of paper and wrinkle it up into a ball, being careful not to rip it.
2. Open up the paper but don't smooth it out. It should look somewhat topographic, like a bird's-eye view of mountains and valleys.
3. Place it in box or on a drop cloth to prevent over-spray damaging other surfaces. Be sure you have good ventilation.

Materials for spray paint "tie dye": wrinkled paper, spray paint, 3-sided box

4. Spray the paint from a diagonal direction onto the paper. The paint will collect on the sides and tops of the "mountains."
5. If you want a second color, approach the paper from another diagonal position and spray.
6. When finished and the paper is completely dry, iron the sheet flat.
7. *Tips*: A flat spray paint paired with a metallic is an interesting contrast. Light colors sprayed onto dark colored paper (e.g. good quality construction paper) makes a dramatic sheet. Natural, earthy colors (olive green, brown, etc.) sprayed onto wrinkled kraft paper can give a camouflage look.

Wrinkled paper is sprayed from one diagonal direction.

8. *Tips*: If you want to use this technique for book pages, try masking off a portion of the wrinkled paper with some Post-it® notes and then use the spray paint. The masked-off section will be open for text.

Two sheets of sprayed paper, one with a masked area.

Paper Weaving, Piercing, & Sewing

As in fabric weaving, strips of contrasting paper can be woven together to create a textured page on which text can be written or collaged. Piercing paper also adds texture, with the additional possibility of creating "holes" which reveal something collaged to the back of the pierced page or material on a subsequent page. Attaching other pieces of paper by sewing (rather than pasting) provides visual interest, additional texture, and a special handmade quality. All of these methods are ways of revealing or concealing content.

> **Materials:**
> - X-acto or razor knife
> - cutting mat or heavy cardboard
> - any weight paper
> - strips of paper, ribbon, fiber, raffia, etc. for weaving
> - scissors
> - thick needle, pin tool, or fine awl
>
> 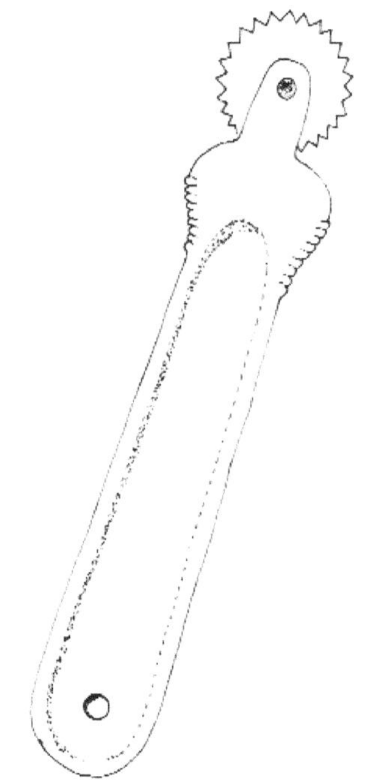
>
> - pattern-marking tool (serrated wheel)
> - glue stick and/or clear tape
> - needles and threads of various weights

Directions:

For weaving, cut parallel strips into paper, beginning and ending about 1" from any edge.

1. With a loose strip of paper, fiber, etc., alternate one horizontal strip over the first vertical strip and then under the next vertical strip, and so on.
2. To secure strips so they will not unravel, use tape (if the back won't be seen) or discrete dabs of glue. You could also sew the ends with thread.
3. For the purposes of creating environment for artist book pages, consider the following possibilities:
   - use strips of different widths and lengths
   - include other materials: fiber, wire, sticks, bark, lace, etc.
   - weave diagonally instead of in a square or rectangular layout
   - write on selected squares after plain strips are woven
   - weave together strips of two different but relating texts
4. Paper weaving works well as a collage element. Try adhering text or images or even transparencies over portions of the woven piece.

For piercing, you are removing a bit of paper ranging from the size of a pin-hole to that of a small window or door going through the page.

1. Working on a cutting mat or piece of dense cardboard, poke holes with a needle tool or slice openings with a razor knife. If you intend to reveal information or an image from the next page, some planning will need to be done (e.g. use tracing paper overlays to position the opening).
2. A pattern wheel or serrated wheel (found with sewing supplies) gives a "path" of dotted holes when rolled over a sheet of paper that is cushioned from beneath. Place your paper on a stack of paper towels or newspaper to get this effect. *Do not run the serrated wheel off the page or your paper will tear along this line.*

3. Another way to get a continuous line of pierced holes is to run the paper through a sewing machine without using thread.
4. Some ideas with piercing: sew through the holes with thread or other fibers; cut windows or doors leaving the flaps for opening and closing to make the page interactive with its audience; combine piercing with weaving for a multi-layered effect.
5. *Tips*: To pierce regularly spaced or geometric patterns, tape your page to a sheet of graph paper and pierce through the two sheets. When finished remove the graph paper.

For sewing, you are attaching separate pieces by means of stitching, whether it is hand-stitched or machine sewn. This technique can be used on squares of paper; pieces of cloth at-

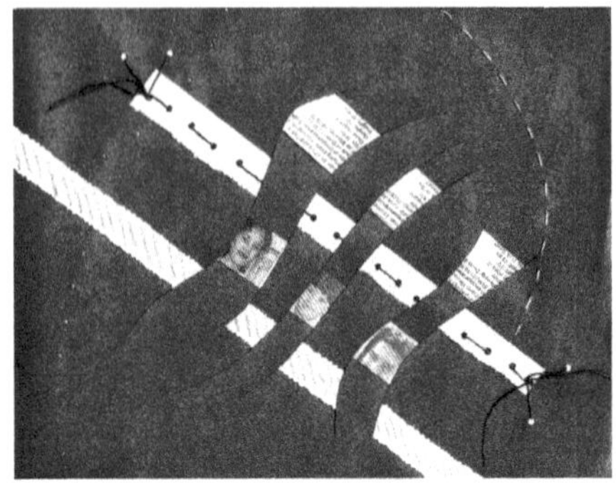

A sheet that has been
pierced, sewn, and woven

tached to paper pages; twigs, feathers, leaves, and other 3-dimensional (but relatively flat) objects that you want to include on a page.

1. *Tips*
    - Make sure that whatever you are sewing is not too heavy to be supported by the page to which it will be attached.
    - If you don't like the look of the stitching on the reverse of the page, back the page with another sheet of paper (pasted on).
    - To stabilize the piece that's being sewn onto the page, dab it with a glue stick, just so it will stay put as you are sewing.
    - Pure cotton or linen thread is better to use on paper than polyester thread, which is stronger and has a better chance of ripping the paper. Whenever you are sewing paper, whether for collage or in binding, *always pull your thread in the direction that you are sewing.* If you yank it, even gently, in the opposite direction to tighten your stitches, the paper will rip!

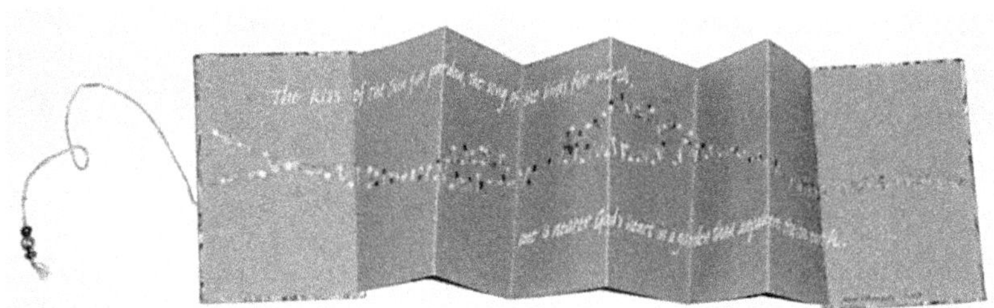

"The Garden," by Meg Kennedy, 2003. Embroidered accordion book.

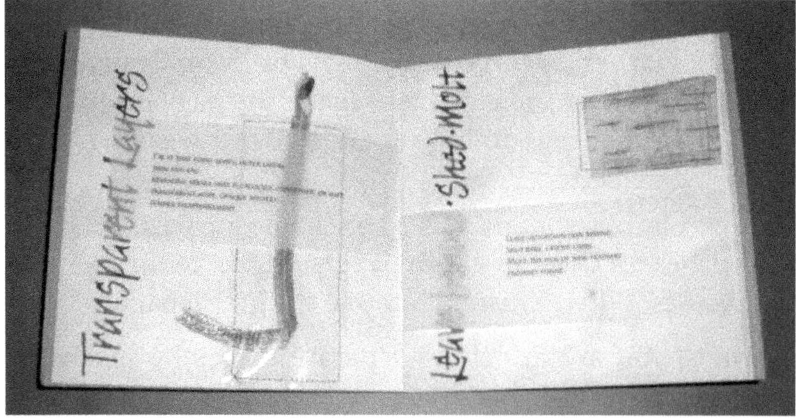

From "Shedding," by Meg Kennedy, 2005.
Snakeskin and birch bark sewn onto pages.

Bubble Marbling

This method of imprinting colored bubbles onto paper can create a delicate, ethereal background or a densely colored, textural stage for words and images. The first time I tried this, using purple ink, the bubbles looked like hydrangea blossoms so I used it as a floral background for text about gardening.

Blow bubbles until they mound up over the top of the container.

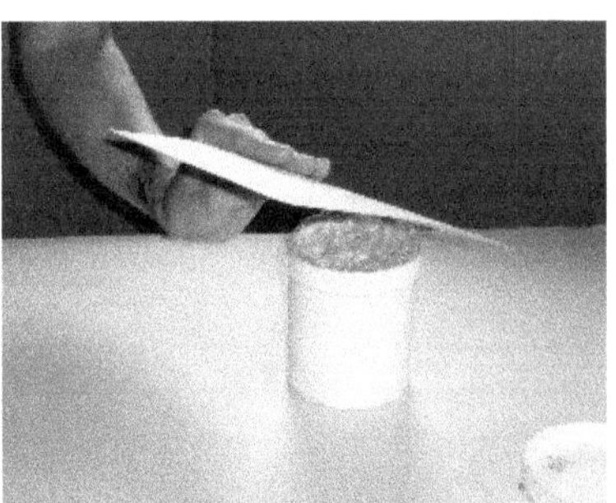

Printing bubbles

Bubble marbled paper that was masked off with a Post-it® note.

Directions:

1. Mix together 2 parts detergent to 1 part water to 1 part pigment in a container no wider in diameter than a coffee can but not as deep (the bubbles have to mound up over the top of the container).
2. With a straw, blow bubbles until they mound up above the rim of the container.
3. Lay paper lightly on top of bubbles and remove: small colored outlines of bubbles are printed on the paper.
4. Do this repeatedly (blow bubbles, print paper, blow bubbles, print paper, etc.) until desired area is filled with overlapping bubble patterns.
5. You can print two or more colors on top of each other for a rich, denser pattern.
6. *Tip*: After the sheet is dry, you can use colored pencils to enhance the design, accentuating or redefining certain areas.

Materials:

- water
- water-soluble ink or paint (intense colors are best)
- clear dish detergent or bubble soap
- short container with opening no wider than 4″
- straws (at least one per person so as not to spread germs)
- medium- to heavy-weight paper
- a rack or place for paper to dry flat
- optional: finely-ground glitter to add to the pigment

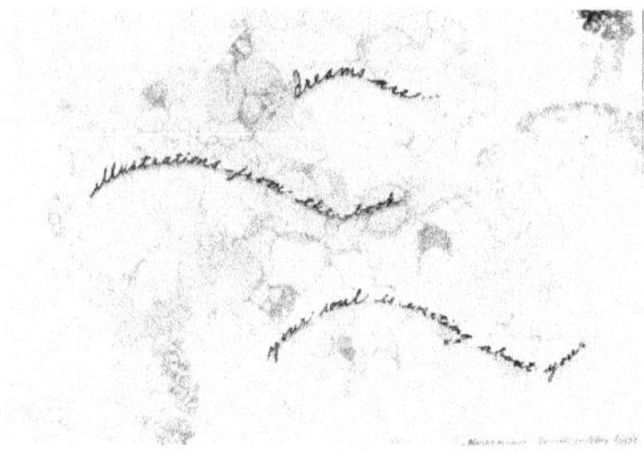

Text written on bubble marbling.

Chalk Marbling

The delicate swirling colors from chalk marbling give a soft background for a bolder graphic or textual message. This technique also can be used to create decorative paper for covers, provided several coats of spray fixative are applied.

Materials for chalk marbling: pan of water, X-acto knife, colored drawing chalk, stick for swirling patterns.

Materials:

- colored artist chalk (not blackboard chalk)*
- straight-edged razor blade or X-acto® knife
- dishpan of tap water, half full
- medium- to heavy-weight paper
- bamboo skewer or other thin stick
- place for marbled paper to dry
- workable spray fixative (need ventilation)

* I've always used Crayola Colored Drawing Chalk, but other brands of drawing chalk, as well as sidewalk chalk (pale results) and hard pastels, will work. What you don't want to use is the colored chalk that can be used on blackboards.

Directions:

1. Gently scrape a stick of colored chalk over a pan of water so that the colored particles float on the water. More than one color should be used.
2. When you have enough color on the water, *gently* make swirling or wavy patterns with a stick or skewer. If you stir too vigorously, the pigment will drop to the bottom of the water.
3. Lay a piece of paper onto the water surface and lift paper off. The chalk pattern will be imprinted on the paper.
4. Once the paper is dry, apply spray fixative to prevent smearing.
5. *Tips*: try printing a second sheet to get a ghost image of the first. Change water after every few sheets of paper to get cleaner prints.

Chalk is gently scraped with a razor blade so that chalk dust floats onto the surface of the water.

Colors are gently swirled with a stick.

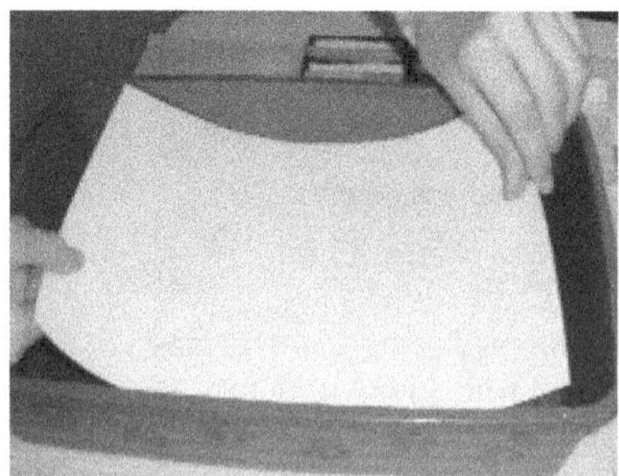
Paper is "bellied" down onto the water surface.

If you want to print both sides of the paper, wait until the first side is dry and coated with a light spray of fixative.

Printed paper is lifted from the surface of the water.

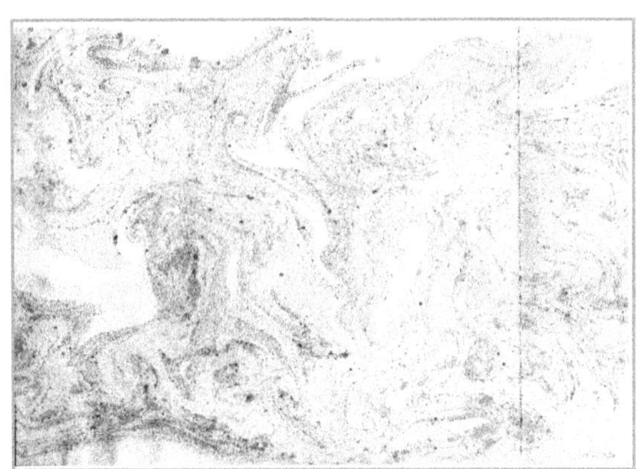

Suminagashi Marbling

The delicate, smoke-like patterns from suminagashi marbling make a wonderful background or stage for content that is magical, mysterious, cloudy, or confusing. Text can be "curled" around the swirling patterns, placed in the white areas that have been left, or written on a transparent overlay that allows the marbled background to be seen. After the paper is dry, you can re-define or emphasize certain areas of the design with colored pencils or even watercolors (Sumi ink dries waterproof). I only use black Sumi ink, but if you can find Sumi ink in colors, that works as well.

Materials for suminagashi marbling: glass tray with approximately 1" of water, Photo Flo™ mixture, Sumi ink, 2 jars with small pointed brushes.

Materials:

- 2 small jars
- liquid Sumi ink
- Photo Flo™ (a surfactant available at any camera shop)
- 2 small watercolor brushes with fine points
- any weight paper
- torn strips of newspaper
- large glass baking dish with about 1-2″ water
- bamboo skewer, drinking straw or paper fan
- place for marbled paper to dry

Directions:

1. In a small jar, make a mixture of 1 tsp. water and 1 drop of Photo Flo™. I usually use two tablespoons of water and 6 drops of Photo Flo™. In another jar put a small amount of Sumi ink.
2. Use one paintbrush for the ink and the other for the Photo Flo™ mixture; *do not mix the brushes.*
3. With a brush in each hand, place a drop of ink onto the water in the pan and allow it to spread. Then place a drop of Photo Flo™ in the center of the ink circle; the ink will be "chased" by the surfactant. Continue with a drop of ink, drop of Photo Flo™ mixture, in a bull's-eye pattern.

Ink and Photo Flo™ mixture alternately placed on the surface of the water with brushes.

Ink pattern is ready to print.

4. To create a pattern from these concentric circles, move a stick *gently* through the water, blow across the surface of the water with the straw, or create a soft breeze over the water with a fan.
5. Lay paper down onto the surface of the water, holding diagonal corners and setting it down "belly first" to minimize bubbles.
6. Lift paper and dry.
7. Between prints, skim ink off surface of the water with torn newspaper.
8. Periodically change the water when it gets too cloudy.

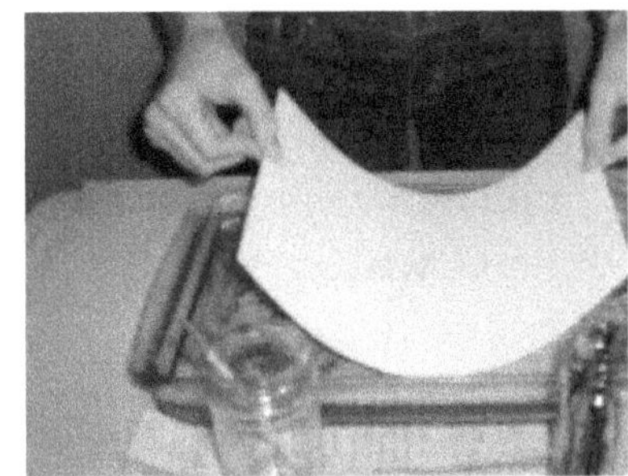

Paper is "bellied" down onto the water surface.

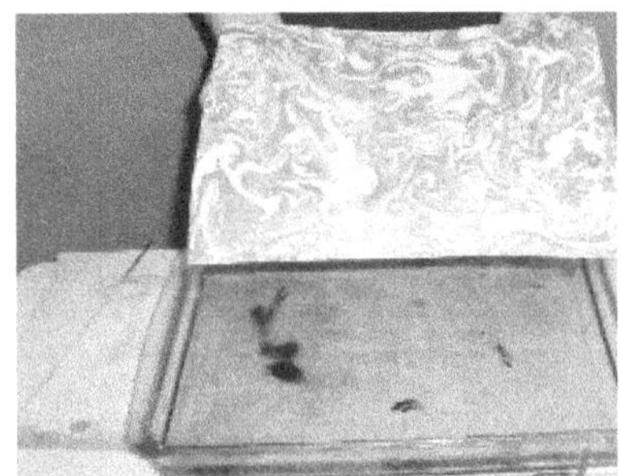

Printed paper is lifted from the surface of the water.

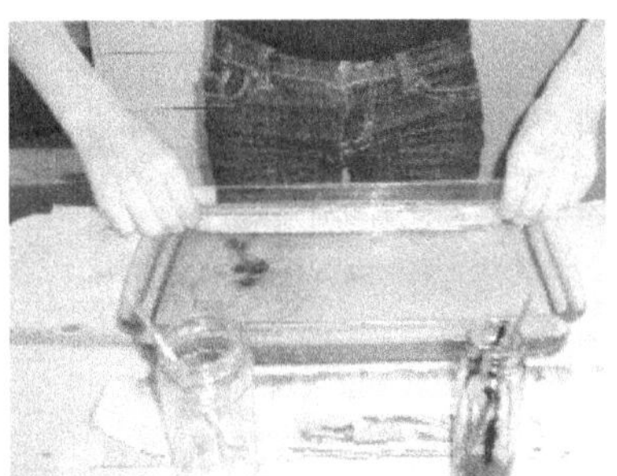

Ink is skimmed off the water with a strip of newspaper.

Paste Papers

Treating paper with colored paste pre-dates the printing press and allowed medieval artists to decorate the endsheets of their hand-written volumes. Paste papers were also used to back and frame delicate Persian and Indian illuminated pieces. With such an auspicious history, however, essentially it is finger-painting for grown-ups. There are many recipes for the paste,* and, in fact, there are books written on the subject. For our purposes, I'm recommending the simplest method which uses a readily available papier mâché powder that school art rooms often have on hand.

Materials:

- Papier Mâché Art Paste (brand name: Elmer's)
- large wide-mouthed container of water
- several smaller containers for different colors
- either acrylic paint *or* water-color (or gouache, finely ground tempera, etc.) + acrylic matte medium (to make the color waterproof)
- medium- to heavy-weight paper
- tools to pattern paste (e.g. Popsicle sticks, plastic fork, comb, rubber spatula)
- place for paste paper to dry (clothes line or rack)

Directions:

1. Mix the Elmer's Art Paste with water in the following proportions: 2 teaspoons of powdered paste to one cup of water. (Don't follow the directions on the box; they are for papier mâché and make a paste that's too thin for paste papers.)
2. Fill several small containers with a few tablespoons of paste and some paint (the concentration of paint will determine the density of color). Mix well. If you are using watercolors, add about a teaspoon of acrylic matte medium to each container. This makes your finished paste paper waterproof and smear-proof.

Materials for painting papers with colored paste: 2 pots of paste mixed with pigment, water jar for cleaning brushes, natural sponge and combing tool for making patterns, wide brush and paper.

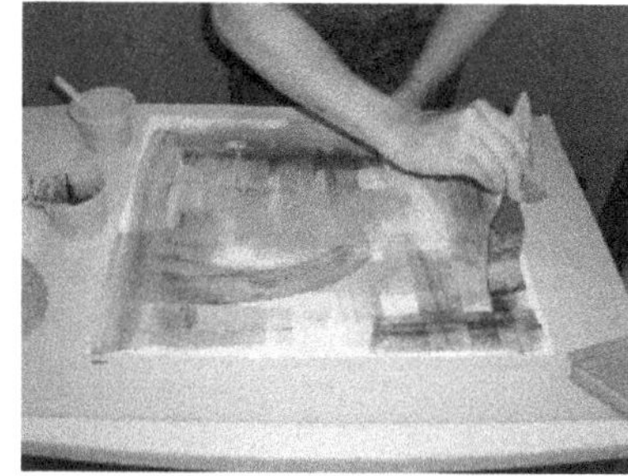

Paste is painted onto paper.

* The traditional method for making paste paper involves rice flour paste that is cooked. This and other recipes for making paste yield beautiful results, but the one described above is easier.

3. This is a messy project, so you might want to tape a large plastic garbage bag to the surface of your work table. After you are finished making paste papers, you can throw away the plastic and have a clean table.

Pattern is combed into the wet paste.

4. Depending on the weight of the paper you are using and the liquidity of your paste mixture, you can either dampen paper with a sponge, spritz it with a spray bottle of water, or apply the colored paste to dry paper. I've had all of these methods work well.

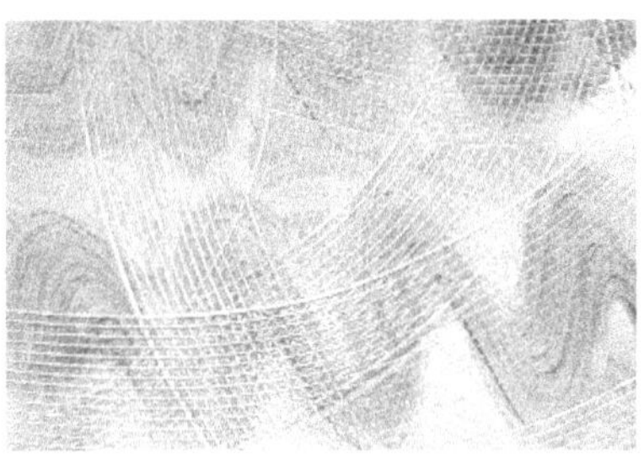

Paste Paper painted and combed.

5. Apply colored paste with a brush or sponge onto the paper. Move the paste around with hands, brush, sponge, or other mark making tools (e.g. comb, fork, stick, etc.). Several colors can be applied to a sheet, but be careful not to make mud. Work gently; the paste-dampened paper is fragile when wet.
6. Let sheet dry, flat if possible, or hung from a clothes line. The other side of the sheet can be done once the first side is dry.

Spread from "Making Marks," by Meg Kennedy, 2005.
Paste-painted pages.

Nature Printing

For years, botanists have used nature printing to record and illustrate accurately the detail of plants. As an art form, nature printing involves complex methods of inking, layering, masking out, and combining diverse elements into an aesthetic whole. As a background or an illustration, however, a nature print couldn't be easier. The simplest method is to use colored stamp pads, but water-soluble printing inks—which most school art rooms keep in stock—give better results.

Materials:

- leaves or other vegetation, pressed or freshly picked
- medium- to light-weight paper that is absorbant (not glossy)
- scrap paper (e.g. unprinted newsprint)
- cosmetic sponges
- either water-soluble printing ink (tubes), brayers, glass or plastic plates or small stamp pads

Directions:

Materials for nature printing: leaves; stamp pad; printing ink, brayer, and plexiglas; wooden spoon and paper

Leaf is inked with a brayer.

Inked leaf is laid down onto the paper.

1. Unless you are going to pick a leaf and print it immediately, you should plan on pressing the specimens you want to print. An easy way to do this is to use an old phonebook, interleave the plants in pages, and put weight (e.g. another heavy book) on top of the closed phonebook. The cheap paper in the phonebook will absorb moisture and help the plants to dry out. Alternatively, lay the plants (leaves, flowers, grasses, etc.) on a sheet of waxed paper, cover with another sheet of waxed paper, and cover this with a sheet of cardboard (non-corrugated) or wood. Put weight on top of this as well. Plan ahead: it will take at least 24 hours for the plants to be sufficiently pressed for printing.
2. *If using printing ink*: squeeze out a toothpaste-sized dollop

of ink onto the plate (or use 2-3 colors for a variegated effect) and roll out a thin sheet of color with a brayer. Roll the inked brayer over the side of the leaf you wish to print (the side with veins creates more detailed prints). Do not over-ink; your print will smear.

3. *If using stamp pads*: select your colors and dab them onto the surface of the leaf that you want printed.
4. Whether using printing ink or stamp pads, carefully pick up the inked leaf (this is where the tweezers come in handy) and lay it, ink side down, onto the sheet of paper that you want printed.
5. Cover the leaf with a piece of clean scrap paper and carefully press the inked leaf onto the page, using your fingers, a clean brayer, or the bowl of a spoon. It's important not to move the leaf so that you get a clear impression and not a smudged one.
6. Lift the leaf and re-ink for the next print, or select another piece of vegetation to print and start again.
7. *Tips*: Before re-inking the leaf, try making a "ghost print," another faint impression. Try printing both sides of a leaf: two versions of the same shape. Overlap prints using different colors to give more depth to a page. As in stenciling, it's more interesting to run a print

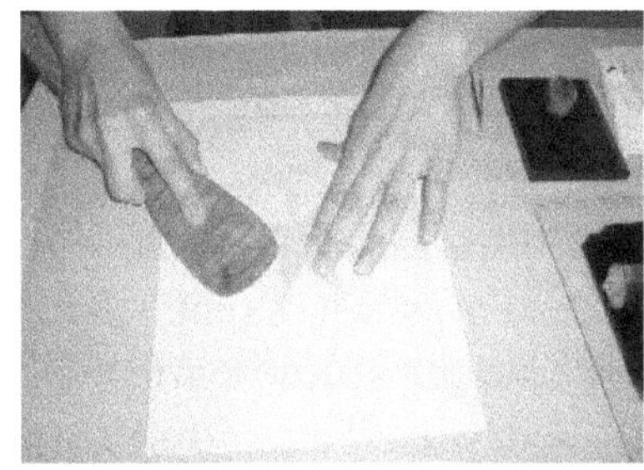

Covered with an extra sheet of paper, the leaf is rubbed gently with the wooden spoon.

Leaf is removed with a tweezers to reveal the print.

Leaf is inked with a small stamp pad.

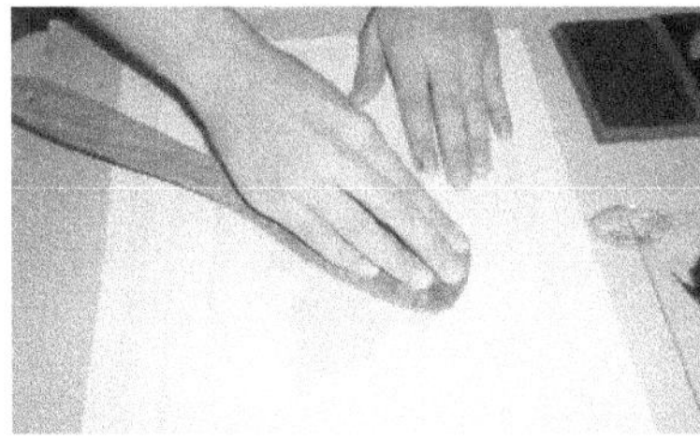

Covered with paper, the leaf is rubbed with the wooden spoon.

off the page instead of just "plunking it down in the middle"!

8. One last suggestion: remember that these prints are water soluble and will run if exposed to moisture. If you want to add a watercolor wash, or another water-based technique, spray the printed page with workable fixative to seal it.

Leaf prints, using a stamp pad.

Watercolor Washes with Alterations:

Salt & Alcohol Resist, Plastic Wrap Crystals, & Masking

You don't have to be a watercolor artist to use this medium effectively. A "wash" is achieved by wetting the entire sheet of watercolor paper and touching one or more colors into the wet surface. The colors will bleed together in an atmospheric way. (This is often how "real" artists get dramatic skies in their paintings.) Much of what you produce from the following techniques will depend on your selection of colors. Both salt and alcohol resist watercolor. Wrinkled plastic wrap applied to a wet wash attracts, traps, and resists areas of color to create crystal-like patterns. Masking fluid is like thin rubber cement that is painted on in areas where color is not wanted. Artists who depict snow scenes often paint areas that should remain pure white with masking fluid before adding other colors. You can mask out areas on a page to allow for text or other meaningful white space.

Materials:

- watercolor paper (hot press is best; cold press is acceptable; rough is difficult to write on.)
- 2-3 watery mixtures of watercolor
- a brush for each color
- water pot and large clean brush

  or a sink

  or a spray bottle of water
- coarse kosher or sea salt
- rubbing alcohol in spray bottle
- plastic wrap
- masking fluid*
- cheap brush for masking fluid
- soapy water for cleaning brush

* Masking fluid is made by several companies, comes in a small jar or plastic bottle with applicator, and is marketed under such names as Incredible White Mask, Masquepen, Art Maskoid, Miskit Liquid Frisket, Liquid Masque, Colorless Art Masking Fluid.

Directions for watercolor wash with salt & alcohol resist:

1. Another messy project (see paste papers) for which plastic garbage bags may make clean-up easier.
2. Mix a few colors with water and have a brush for each color.
3. Watercolor paper is sprayed or brushed with water or run under a faucet. Wet both sides of the paper so that it won't curl while you are working on it.
4. While the paper is still wet, drop selected colors onto the paper and watch them spread and mix in places. You can

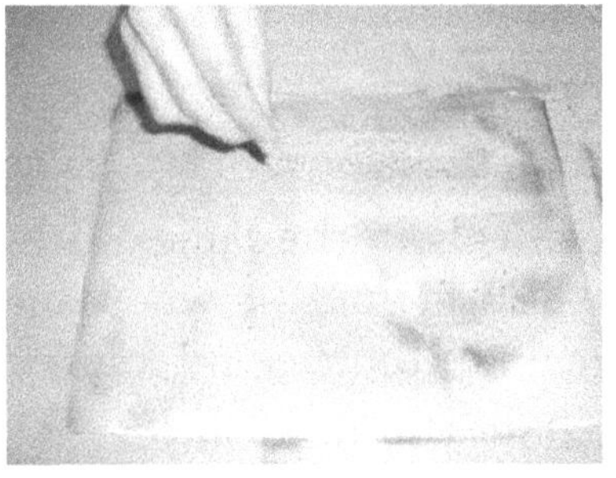

Kosher or sea salt is sprinkled over a wet watercolor wash.

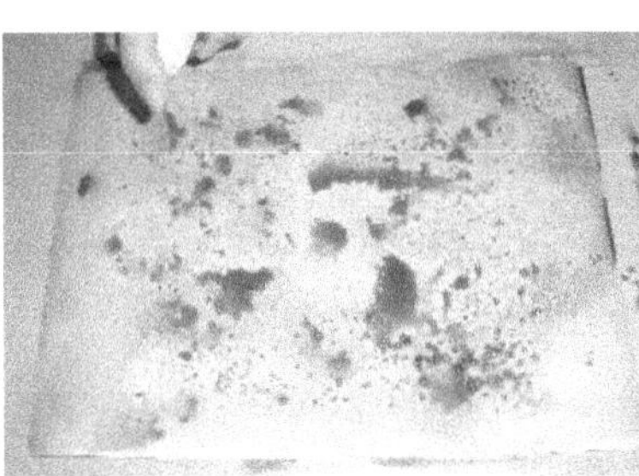

Rubbing alcohol is sprayed onto a wet watercolor wash.

manipulate where they are going with a brush. Deepen the colors by adding more paint.

5. When the colors have settled down a bit, but paper is still wet, sprinkle the paper with salt to make dots of resist. Lightly spray the paper with rubbing alcohol for starburst areas of resist (areas that push away the color).

Directions for watercolor wash with plastic wrap crystals:

1. Paint a watercolor wash on paper as described above.
2. Take a piece of plastic wrap larger than the paper, wrinkle it up, and place it onto the wet paint. The wrinkles in the plastic are what create the crystal-like patterns so don't smooth it out.
3. Set the sheet aside and let it dry. After it's dry, peel up the plastic wrap.
4. This can be done over the salt and alcohol resist with really interesting results.

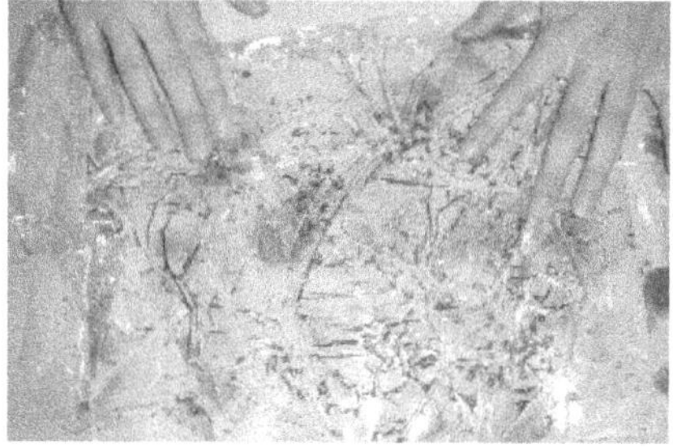

Plastic wrap is wrinkled and pressed onto a wet watercolor surface and allowed to dry.

Directions for watercolor wash with masking:

1. Whichever brand of masking fluid you choose, they all work about the same. With a brush or other tool, apply the masking fluid anywhere on the paper that you want to remain untouched by color.
2. Allow the masking fluid to dry thoroughly, then paint over it with a watercolor wash.
3. When the paint is dry, peel or rub off the masking fluid (or use a rubber cement pick-up).
4. A subtle environment can be created by writing out key words or images with masking fluid, painting or surfacing the paper, removing the mask, and adding text over it. The

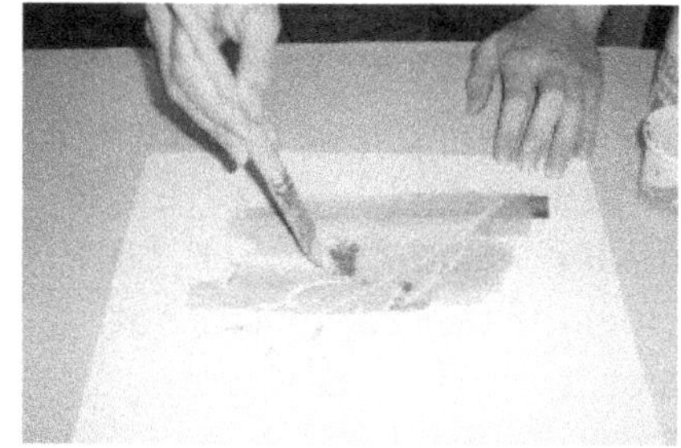

A watercolor wash is painted over an image drawn with masking fluid.

masked words will then suggest messages being revealed through the other layers of surfacing and text.

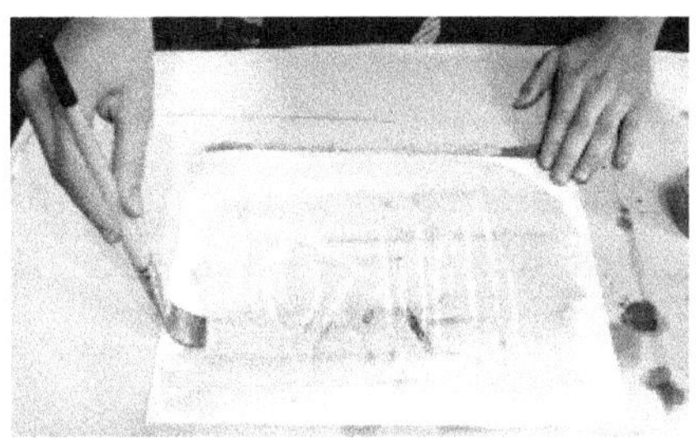

A watercolor wash is painted over a word written with masking fluid.

4. *Tips*: be sure the paper is dry when you apply the masking fluid and let it dry thoroughly before painting over. Immediately clean any tools—brushes, pens—that you dip into masking fluid or they will be permanently ruined. To further protect brushes, dip them into soapy water before dipping into masking fluid.

Spread from "Fire," by Meg Kennedy, 1999.
Pages with watercolor wash, salt and alcohol resist, and plastic wrap crystals.

Final Note:

In addition to these methods for creating visual interest on a page, two other suggestions come to mind, each of which has inspired books on the subject.

- Collage is an effective way to combine thematic elements on a page and can be done with words as well as images.
- Block printing (or rubber stamping) can be a means of illustrating and can also provide a way to unify a series of pages by repeating an image or pattern on each sheet.

Both of these familiar techniques are simpler to describe, however, than to do well. A good sense of design is needed to avoid the dreaded trap of excessive cuteness or mind-numbing repetition.

5 Creating Poetry-Friendly Environments

Just as the visual artist faces the blank page or canvas and may panic, many writers, both students and professionals, often face the blank page with dread. When I enter a classroom as a visiting poet and ask students what makes it hard for them to make a poem, the most common answer I receive is "I never know what to write about or where to start!"[1]

In reality, children are natural poets. In his book on creative process, *Free Play*, Steven Nachmanovitch tells of a second grader who was asked how she defined a negative number. "She said without hesitating, 'It's like looking at your reflection in a pool of water. It goes down as far as you go up.' This is original mind in action."[2] The issue for us as educators is not so much how to teach students to write poetically, but how to draw poetic thoughts and ideas from students, how to get them to express these on the page.

All of us use poetry in our daily language.

All of us use poetry in our daily language. Whenever you say you are so hungry you could eat a horse, you are using figurative language. When you tell a friend about the incident at the store, you select the details that will create tension, momentum and even musicality, and in this way engage your listener: *The woman ahead of me in line had fourteen items at the ten or less check-out, and the checker with the pierced eyebrow started to bite her*

[1] All the tips here apply to any form of creative writing, whether you focus on story writing, essay writing, or poetry itself.

[2] *Free Play*, Steven Nachnamovitch, NY: G.P. Putnam's Sons, 1990

nails like a chipmunk gnawing on glass as the shopper (her kids screaming) piled on that eleventh item.

Poems are most easily educed in a poetry-friendly environment. What follows are some tips I have learned toward creating such an environment. These tips all appear in a brief reminder chart at the end of this section.

Right up front, note for your students the difference between the creator and the editor. I do this by drawing my "poet brain" on the blackboard. I label one side "Genius" and the other "Editor" and separate the two parts with a double line, then explain that both parts need to function for me to make a poem. The catch is if the two parts try to function at exactly the same time, the Editor tends to hop the divider and overwhelm the Genius or Ideas Center. Each half gets to speak, but one at a time. (I like to ask students if they have had this experience: *You really want to tell your friend about something that happened. All the way on the bus ride to school you are trying to think of the name of the person who walked into the store just as this incident was happening. You get to school having recovered the person's name but forgotten the story you were going to tell.* Most students relate to this kind of "over-thinking" of a flash of an idea.)

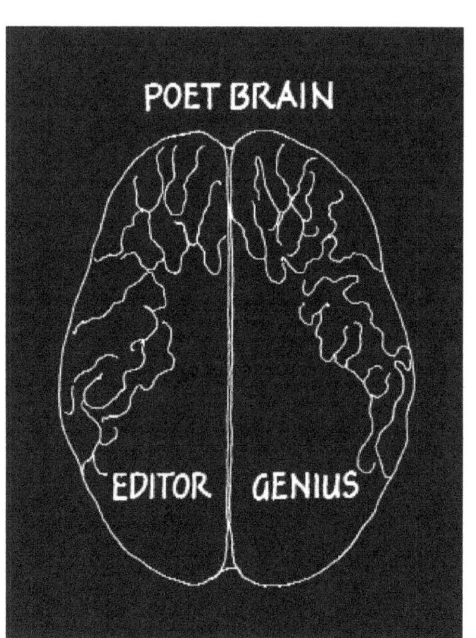

Encourage students to operate in their creator brain and go back and revise once they've captured their genius onto paper. Remind students that precise rhythm, word choice and line breaks can be refined in revision. Revision comes as a second step to grabbing the original thought and getting it onto paper. Polishing comes as a third step after revision. Encourage students to get down the ideas and remind them that what they see in a published poem is unlikely to have been the poet's first draft. A reminder: over-thinking really does create a situation in which good poem ideas are lost.

Along the same lines, set rules that engender safety in getting down these original thoughts: spelling doesn't count until later. No writing about classmates in rude or embarrassing ways. You may need to consider the setting in which the poems are made: no using language (e.g., obscenities) that would be unacceptable to say out loud in this setting. This one is tricky. Sometimes the crude word is the one that fits a character in a monologue or fits the situation. Often, however—and I remind students about this— there is a more precise, interesting, or original way of expressing the emotion carried in the obscenity.

Three steps:

1. Create

2. Revise

3. Polish

As much as possible, talk about poetry in common rather than technical language in order to demystify it. And speaking of demystifying poetry: Remind your students that they use figurative language in everyday speech all the time. *(He was walking like a bear and I knew he was about to growl like one, so I stayed away from him all day.)*

Allow talk and movement during writing time. Art is messy. And the less the teacher "explains" and the more students are left to do, the better. Let lessons emerge from student work.

I try to offer very brief mini-lessons. These involve warm-up exercises. (See below, and rest assured: some will be suggested with each writing prompt). Then I get the students writing. Teachers can share strategies for shaping poems once there are words on the page.

Share strategies for shaping poems once there are words on the page.

Use student examples. Other students are your students' creative peers. They relate to their ideas, feelings and ways of expressing themselves. Books of student work and books that include student examples are listed in our bibliography. When possible, use work from last year's students to inspire this year's students. Offer many examples to students if they seem stuck. Once a prompt is introduced, if they seem ready to write, get out of the way and let them.

Above all, show your own enthusiasm. When reading from published poetry, I have found it best to pick poems I like reading, poems I can read expressively. As all teachers know, your enthusiasm is infectious.

Humor helps too.

I find that for most students I get more response if I start with writing assignments that focus on content, images and feeling; add the element of form and models of published poetry after several opportunities to write without these potentially constricting devices. When you do introduce published poetry, try to pick examples that span varied forms and voices. This helps reinforce the students' awareness that poetry is not only written one way.

A Word About Warming Up

If you walk in and say "We're going to write poems," you are likely to encounter some resistance. Walk in and say, "We're going to get thinking like poets." When I walk into a classroom, I tell students that before we write, we are going to warm up their poet brains. This announcement will be followed by a brief period of playing word games, doing an observation exercise, moving to some guided physical activity or day-dreaming through a guided meditation. Warm-up activities are often noisy, usually laugh-filled, and sometimes involve moving about. I like to remind students that there are "no right answers" as they enter into these games and discussions.

A good warm-up activity will serve to spur the senses and spark the imagination.

Although it is not always necessary to match warm-up activities to the writing prompts which will follow them, I often choose an activity that will not only help loosen inhibitions, but will also demonstrate or illustrate one element of poetry which will be featured in the writing assignment.

For example, when students' poems will center around the use of all five senses, I have popped popcorn and let students create similes about the smell, sound, texture, taste and sight of popcorn kernels. You might have students free associate the connections between objects in the classroom and things that are like them "in one way and no other." (Example: White chalk is like a snowy field.) A way of honing observation skills is to challenge students to look around the familiar classroom and list "ten things I never noticed." (I have had students turn these lists directly into rather interesting poems.)

In the project section, we have included warm-up activities that will lead into the writing prompt piece of each activity. Below are some general warm-up activities. Many good texts exist which include a number of timeless and useful ice breakers. I am indebted to Kenneth Koch[3] for many of the ideas I have found most useful. Over the years I have created some of my own activities, and I have modified others to fit my personal style and my students' needs.

What is important to remember is that students will write more readily and more freely if you give them an opportunity to warm up and play with ideas and words before committing a few chosen words to a structure on the page. A good warm-up activity will serve to spur the senses and spark the imagination. What follows are a few ways to break the ice in your writing workshop.

Summary: Tips for Writing Environments

- draw out the difference between the creator and the editor
- encourage students to create the first draft strictly from the creator brain
- remind students that precise rhythm, word choice and line breaks can be refined in revision
- rules for the Safety of the Road: Spelling doesn't count in early draft
- another Rule: No writing about classmates in rude and embarrassing ways
- be clear (you're the arbiter here) what language is acceptable to use in this setting
- talk about poetry in common language in order to demystify it
- allow talk and movement during writing time
- don't over-explain; let lessons emerge from student work
- use student examples
- offer many examples to students if they seem stuck
- show your own enthusiasm
- humor helps
- start with a focus on content and move to form later

Some Warm-Up Activities

Journaling

Many teachers of language arts routinely ask their students to keep journals in response to readings or as part of particular classroom activities. When working on poetry projects, you may want to give your students five to ten minutes at the beginning of a writing period to simply write about something they noticed earlier in the same day, or perhaps to recall a dream they had the night before, to verbally explore a feeling for which they are trying to find words, or even just to describe

[3] *Wishes, Lies and Dreams*, Kenneth Koch, N.Y.: Harper & Row, 1970

the view from the classroom window. The important point to keep in mind is that journals need to be safe places to capture and record original thought. Journals should not be evaluated or corrected by a teacher, nor should they be open to public scrutiny unless the writer invites a reader in. A teacher who chooses to ask students to share journals may want to encourage their charges to choose a page or two from this writing to share in private conference. Conference time can be used simply to note where writing is vivid and original. Such comment will encourage the writer to loosen and expand his/her creative thinking.

WORD BOWL

Free Writing

Free writing, like journaling, involves having students simply put pen to page and write without editing. Students may be given a time limit and asked to write nonstop for that time period. If a student can't think of where to begin, or what to write next, encourage him to write "I don't know what to write because" and go from there.

You can give some structure to a free writing period. A word, quotation or phrase on the blackboard can be used as a jumping off place. Bring the students' attention to the word on the board and ask them to write whatever comes to mind about this subject for the time allotted.

Word Bowls: Variations on the Free-Write Theme

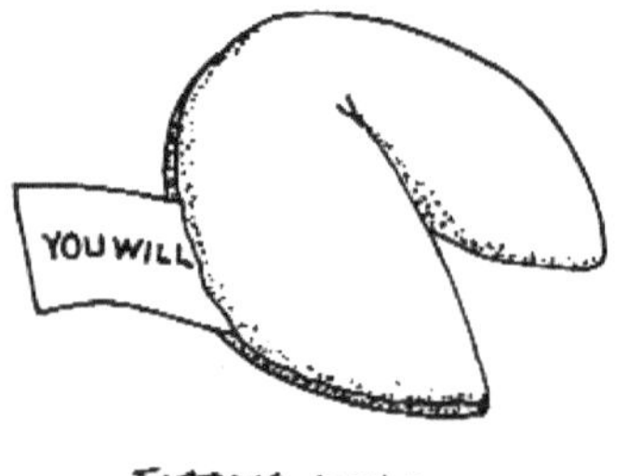

FORTUNE COOKIE

A variation of this guided free write activity is the Word Bowl. Words on squares of construction paper or folded like Chinese fortunes can be placed in a fish bowl. Rather than all students writing from the same word, each student picks a word from the fish bowl and uses that word as the trigger for a free write.

Other variations on this warm-up activity are legion. Try bringing Chinese fortune cookie fortunes and have each student select one from a bowl. Write whatever comes to mind when that fortune is read. Write about a day when that fortune comes true or fails to come true. Have students pick several words from a word bowl and ask them to use all of them in their free writing, or let students give each other words or phrases or quotes as triggers.

Writing from Photos or Postcards

A variation of the word bowl as warm-up activity involves using visual imagery as a writing trigger. Ask each student to bring a postcard into class and have students randomly draw from each other's cards and write about the card chosen. Any number of directions may spark writing about the image. The student can simply describe what is seen; the simple action of putting words to visual images will warm up the students' verbal image-making machinery. You may want to ask students to stretch their imaginations and write about what might be outside of or beyond the scene depicted. What's behind the mountain in the photograph? Who might live in the house?

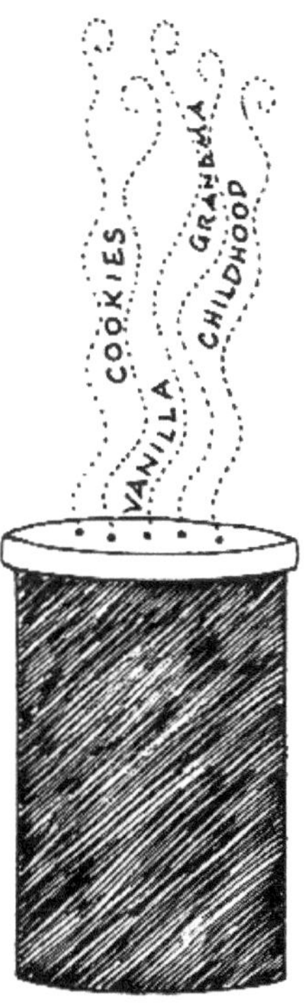

SCENT CANISTER

Using The Other Senses

Try sound as a trigger. Have students listen to a variety of sounds with their eyes closed. You might want to have them write down what color each sound would be if it were painted on a canvas. You might want to have them pick a feeling that goes with that sound.

Scent is a powerful trigger for memory writing. Save film canisters. Fill a few with distinctive scents: vanilla or oregano, fresh mown grass or tobacco. Have students sniff the contents of the canister and then write what place, holiday, person, season, or feeling is brought to mind by that scent. Any association can be developed into a longer piece of writing.

Use of Music and Movement

Music and movement bring rhythm from the thinking brain into the feeling body. Have students listen to music without lyrics either before or while they write. Vary the rhythm of musical selections and have students discuss what mental imagery each rhythm evokes. This is a good time to remind students there are no right answers. When listening to a slow, dirge-like rhythm, some students will "see" a dark, spooky night and others will "see" early dawn and a ribbon of sunlight just appearing on a horizon.

Act or clap out rhythms that would fit different scenarios. Think of a basketball game. Have students move as players on a winning team might move off the court. Then have them move as players might move if they were on the losing team. Clap out the sound a poem about meeting a new friend would make. Then clap out the sound a poem should make if the student were to write about the friend moving away.

> **An Example of a List Poem:**
> (Pulled from student responses given in varied schools)
>
> ***Things I Never Noticed in My Classroom***
>
> *That crack in the ceiling that looks like a river*
> *The extra outlet under the science table*
> *The red marker splotch on the wall*
> *How loud the tick of the clock gets minutes*
> *before lunch*
> *How hard my chair feels after a long test*
> *The way Mrs. Jones pulls her eyebrows into a*
> *vee when she's about to pounce*

Sometimes even taking a stretch can be a good warm-up before sitting and writing. For any artist, getting into one's body can be a good way of getting into a body of work.

Making Lists

Any list can become a poem and list-making can always warm up a writer's brain. Students can walk around the room and list "things I never noticed." List anything: hairstyles I have worn; songs I love or hate; favorite foods; objects needed to play a game of baseball.

Observation: My Mother's Tray Game

As the mother of four active, chatty daughters, my mother became an expert at creating cooling down as well as warming up games. When participants at a birthday party or in a Brownie Scout troop became a bit unfocused, she often hauled out her tray of hidden objects. Ten or twelve small, provocative objects were placed on a tray and covered. We children sat in a circle, and the tray was set in the middle of the circle. No one could move or talk while the cover was removed for thirty seconds and the objects were revealed. We studied the objects intently. Then the cover was replaced while we scrambled to private corners of the room to write down a list of as many of the objects as each of us could recall having seen.

In a classroom you might want to ask students to observe the tray for a brief period and then describe in as much detail as possible the objects observed. Have the students compare notes on which objects they noticed and what each noticed about each object. This is a great opportunity for a teacher to reinforce the power of specific detail in writing. The activity is fun and focuses the energies of most students. It can also be extended into related writing projects. Students can, for example, write in more detail about one of the objects, picture the room from which an object might have come, or simply use the list to create yet another list poem.

A Word About the Power of Limits

While most of these tips seem to suggest that keeping the environment loose and the rules for writing few while poetry is being created, imposing some limits on the writing environment will allow students to create more freely. The blank page is intimidating to us all. Some structure—a starting place and one or two rules for proceeding—allows students to vault past the anxiety created by the blank page and begin writing. These rules could be as simple as offering a broad topic and then setting a time limit (*We'll write for 10 minutes about our neighborhoods and then share our first thoughts*). Each prompt in this volume offers this limited, flexible structure for the creation of student work.

Imposing some limits on the writing environment will allow students to create more freely.

6 Book-Making 101: Just the Basics

There are hundreds of instructional books about making books, so this chapter will give a general overview of materials, tools, and three basic bindings: accordion, pamphlet, and stab binding. By all means, gather some "how to" books on bookbinding and make them available to your students. Seeing examples of handmade volumes will help them generate and nourish ideas for their own books. Meanwhile, the following will get you started.

Materials & Tools

Paper

Unless you are using handmade paper for your books, you will have to understand about *the grain of the paper*, or the direction in which the paper fibers are aligned. When paper is machine-made, it rolls along a type of conveyor belt and the paper fibers run parallel to the length of the belt. Since we don't know where our particular piece of paper was in terms of placement on the conveyor belt, we have to test it to determine the grain. It's easy to tell with cardstock, a little less easy with text weight paper. Take a piece of cardstock and flex it, as though you were going to fold it in half, first horizontally and then vertically. You will be able to feel that there is less resistance in one of those two directions. The lesser resistance indicates the direction of the grain; i.e. if it's easier to fold vertically, the grain runs parallel to the length of the paper. This is more important with heavier weight paper than with thin bond that might be used for pages. If you fold against the grain, especially with heavy paper (e.g. drawing paper), the book may not

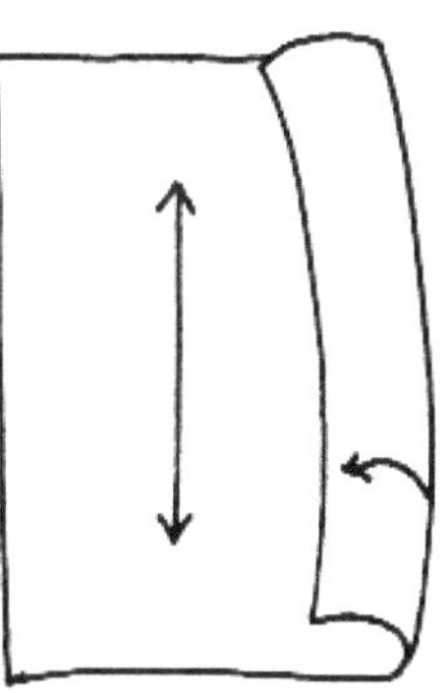

Paper rolls more easily in the direction of the grain.

rest flat (the pages are springing open), or the fold may crack. You've undoubtedly noticed when folding a piece of cardboard that sometimes the crease is neat and straight and other times it's messy and irregular: blame the grain. Fortunately, if you buy a ream of paper of whatever kind, the direction of the grain is the same throughout the package.

There's lots of talk about using *archival materials*, and that's fine if you can afford it. Acid-free paper is generally more expensive, but the good news is that it's now more available as a result of the recent scrap-booking craze. A rule of thumb for all art projects is to use the best materials you can, but not to let uncertainty about the archival qualities of your materials interfere with your creativity. If the resulting piece of work doesn't last fifty years, so be it.

Decorative paper for covers and endsheets is wonderful to work with, but can be expensive. Encourage students to produce their own decorative paper using the various paper surfacing techniques in Chapter 4. Sometimes purchased wrapping paper is a less expensive alternative, but make sure it has a matte surface and is fairly thick (for wrapping paper). The thin, glossy paper sold on rolls for wrapping gifts stretches, tears, wrinkles, and rolls up when coated with glue.

Bookbinding can involve lots of glue, so large quantities of *scrap paper* will be needed. In my experience, the only kinds of scrap paper that do not work well are newspaper and phonebooks. The cheap ink runs when wet with the glue and then stains your book. For smaller projects, I save the many dozens of mail order catalogs that I receive to use as scrap paper. The glossy color doesn't come off, they are plentiful, and you can't beat the price. For larger projects, get a supply of unprinted newsprint (your local newspaper might have ends of rolls they'd be willing to donate) or accumulate and cut open brown paper bags. It's important for each student to have a stack of scrap paper to use, so that they are always working on a clean surface.

Boards

Boards that are used for book covers can be matboard, chipboard, illustration board, bristol board, binders' board, or even actual wood. Do not use corrugated cardboard or posterboard; they both warp when glued. For small books, matboard is sufficient, and often can be obtained from a local picture framer who is more than happy to donate scraps (the insides of mats) for school projects. Chipboard comes in a variety of weights and surfaces, and can be purchased in bulk fairly cheaply. If you intend to cover the board with decorative paper or bookcloth, make sure your board is at least 1⁄16″ to 1⁄8″ thick. In chipboard, this translates to 14-ply to 30-ply. Here's the rule of thumb: the bigger the book, the thicker the board, to insure that your covers won't warp. Finally, if you are planning to cover the boards with a very light color or sheer paper, you will need to use white illustration, mat, or bristol boards. Brown or gray chipboards will show through the paper when pasted.

Glue and Paste

Book artists usually use a combination of PVA (polyvinyl adhesive, i.e. white glue) and methyl cellulose (wallpaper paste). The PVA dries quickly and the methyl cellulose slows down the drying time. You might ask, "why not just add water to the PVA?" Because it cuts the adhesion of the glue. Since methyl cellulose is a paste, it dilutes the glue with another substance that is an adhesive. Since PVA is far costlier than plain old white glue, I use Elmer's glue in classes, and haven't noticed any difference. To 8 ounces of white glue, add a tablespoon of methyl cellulose. If you buy the methyl cellulose as a powder, just mix a small amount with water, so that it is the consistency of heavy cream, and then add one tablespoon of that mixture to the glue. Apply the glue with a brush. My favorite glue brush is the type of "chunky brush" that companies like Crayola make for children to paint with, but any ½" to 1" stiff bristle brush will do. Make sure to dampen the brush with water before dipping it into the glue; it will be easier to clean after you're finished.

No matter what anybody tells you, glue sticks are not permanent and should not be used for covering boards or assembling parts of the book that are structural. They are fine to use for collage. Never use rubber cement: it's not permanent, has flammable fumes, and causes eventual brown staining of the papers to which it comes in contact.

How to make your own bookcloth:

You will need:

- cloth
- double-stick fusible adhesive web*
- lightweight Japanese paper ("rice paper" sold for Sumi ink drawing comes in rolls and sheets)
- an iron

Steps:

1. Set the iron at the temperature indicated on the fusible web directions.
2. Place the rough side of the web against the wrong side of the fabric.
3. Press for a few seconds and let the fabric cool.
4. Peel off the backing paper from the web and place the Japanese paper over it.
5. Press again.

You have paper-backed fabric, a.k.a. bookcloth!

* The two brands of fusible adhesive web that I've used are: Wonder-Under (a product of Freudenberg Nonwovens, Pellon Division, 119 West 40th Street, New York, NY 10018) and Steam-A-Seam 2 (a product of The Warm Company, 954 East Union Street, Seattle, WA 98122). They are available at fabric stores in the interfacing department.

Bookcloth

The cloth used on the spines of books, and sometimes the entire cover is a cloth that is either backed with paper or impregnated with starch to prevent glue from seeping through and staining the fabric. Bookcloth is sold by various mail order companies (see Resource section) and is sometimes available at art and craft supply stores. It is not very expensive and a yard is enough for several books, but if you want to make your own, see the sidebar at left.

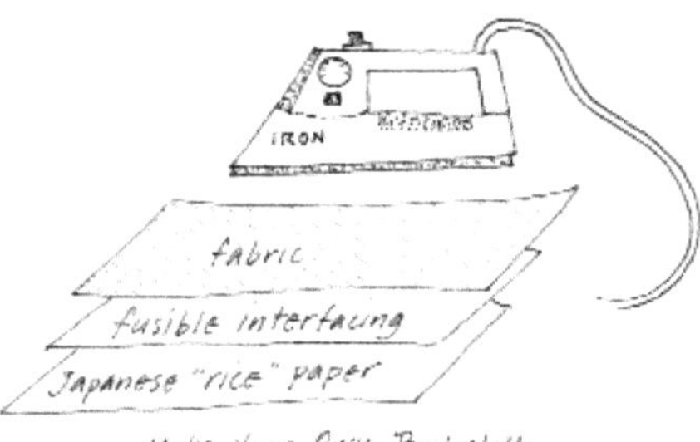

Make Your Own Bookcloth

Bone folder

This essential bookbinding tool resembles a letter opener made out of bone or ivory. It is used for scoring* and smoothing folds, and is, in fact made from animal bone. If you are going to do a significant amount of bookbinding, it's a good idea to obtain bone folders for your class to use. They can be purchased in bulk—10 or more—for about $5.00 apiece (see Resource Section). As an alternative, you can use the blunt end of a bamboo skewer to score a line for a fold, and the bowl of a spoon can smooth the fold. When smoothing a fold with a bone folder, place the tool flat on the paper and move gently across the fold. If you place the tool up on its edge, it will burnish a shiny mark on the paper.

* "Scoring" a fold means to draw an invisible line where you want the paper to fold. Using a bone folder like a pencil, you would "draw" a line against a ruler, which compresses the paper fibers and convinces the paper to crease just there. This is especially useful for heavy weight papers and if you need to fold against the grain of the paper.

Awl

In bookbinding, you measure out where the stitches will be and pierce the holes with an awl, rather than allowing a pointy needle to make random holes. Bookbinders' awls are available from mail order catalogs (see Resource Section) and are narrower in diameter than an awl typically found in a hardware store. A good, and cheaper, substitute is a needle tool used by potters. This tool is available at most art supply stores.

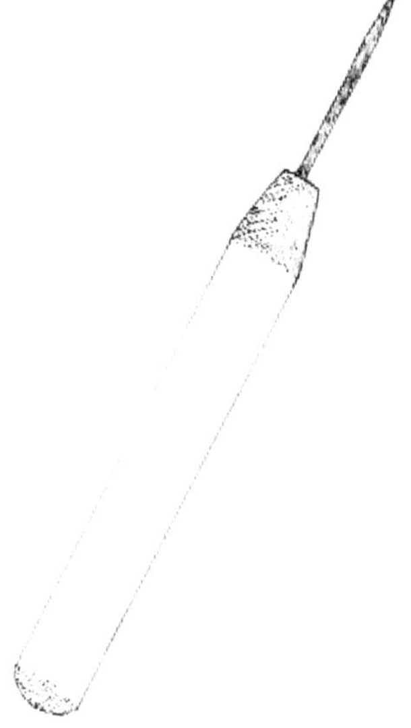

Awl (Potter's Needle Tool)

Needles, Thread, and Beeswax

Bookbinding needles are blunt-ended, since the awl makes the holes for sewing, and are available mainly from mail order catalogs (see Resource Section). As far as I can tell, they are identical to tapestry needles, which come in a variety of sizes and are available wherever sewing notions are found. For most bookbinding projects, needles in sizes 18 – 22 (18 being the larger needle) are sufficient.

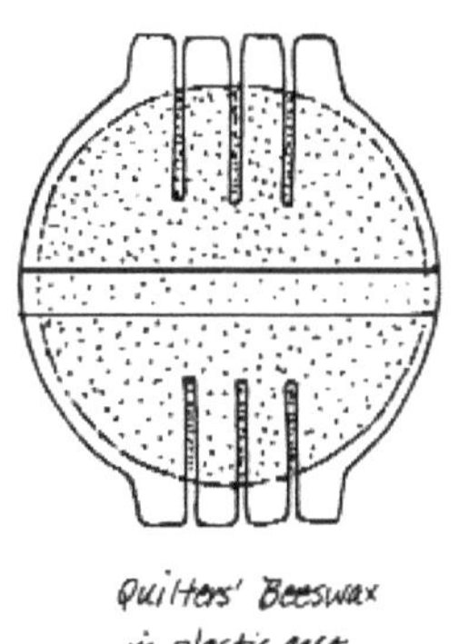

Quilters' Beeswax in plastic case

While it's traditional to use linen thread for binding, cotton crochet thread and DMC cotton needlework twist (#5) are what I prefer for artist's books. They are easy to find in craft stores and where sewing notions are sold, are available in numerous wonderful colors, and are less expensive than linen thread. Do not use spools of thread sold for sewing machine use; this is polyester wrapped in cotton which easily tears paper.

Beeswax is used to coat the thread before sewing with it. The waxy coating provides lubrication, strengthens the thread, and helps to keep final knots from slipping. In medieval times, beeswax also served as an insecticide: since bookworms didn't like the taste, binding stitches weren't chewed.

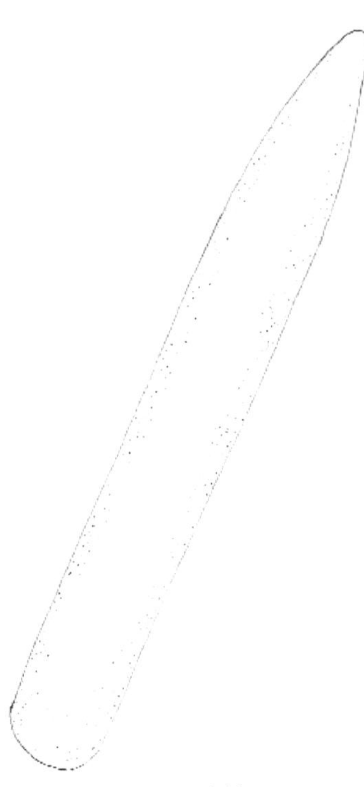

Bone folder

Basic Bookbinding Kit

Throughout the projects, a "basic bookbinding kit" is listed in the materials section. This tool kit contains the following:

- a sharpened pencil
- eraser
- metal-edged ruler
- scissors
- bone folder
- tapestry needle (#18, 20, or 22)
- beeswax
- cotton or linen thread
- X-Acto® knife and extra blades
- cutting mat or heavy cardboard
- awl or pottery needle tool
- glue brush
- glue
- 2 spring-type clothespins

Most of these materials have already been described. The X-Acto® knife, blades, and cutting mat are needed for cutting cover boards and trimming pages. Always cut against a metal or metal-edged ruler. The clothespins are used for holding a gathering of pages open while you are sewing them, acting somewhat like a third hand.

A Few Basic Techniques

Accuracy

When measuring and marking materials for folding or cutting, accuracy is important both for structure and aesthetics. This is where book arts and math skills intersect. Emphasize the old adage, "measure twice, cut once," and allow enough time for students to give complete attention to this activity.

Here are a few tips for increased accuracy:

- Use the same ruler throughout an entire project. To my surprise, I've found slight variations among rulers! Some rulers start in about ¼″ from the edge. Alert students to this possibility; if they have a ruler like this and start measuring from the end of the ruler, all of their measurements will be off by that amount, no matter how careful they are.
- When giving dimensions, always give the width first and then the height (e.g. 5×7″ means 5″ wide by 7″ high)
- There are two ways to mark measurements for scoring or cutting: (1) measure from one edge of the paper or board at the top (and make a dot) and at the bottom (and make a dot), and then, with a ruler aligned with the two dots, draw a line, make a cut, or score a fold. Or, (2) measure from one edge of the paper or board and make a dot. Hook a T-square onto a perpendicular edge and line it up with the measurement mark. You can then draw a line, make a cut, or score a fold.
- When marking a measurement, use a very sharp, hard pencil. The width of a dull pencil point could throw off a measurement by 1⁄16″ (which quickly multiplies each time you use that blunt pencil).
- Alternatively, when marking a measurement for cutting, use an awl to puncture a small pinpoint hole. The point of the X-Acto® knife can start and stop easily in these hole markings.

Neatness counts

No matter how original or profound the concept being explored in an artist's book, globs of glue seeping through and staining the cover, loose, sloppy stitching, misaligned pages, smears and smudges all distract from the final product (unless it's a book about mess!). It's important to emphasize to students that bookmaking is both an art and a craft; fine craftsmanship involves rules, specific techniques, and traditional as well as innovative forms. In addition to accuracy in measuring, marking, cutting, and folding, neatness counts toward the success of a project.

A few tips on working neatly:

- Have each student bring in two old washcloths to keep with their bookmaking supplies. One should be damp and the other dry. Place these within easy reach of your work area so that each time you touch a surface that has been glued, you can dab your fingers on the washcloths (wet, then dry), and continue to work with clean hands.
- Make sure every student has a pile of scrap paper on which to work. The paper should be larger than the sheets being brushed with glue. Each time a piece of scrap paper is used, fold it over to provide a clean surface and either drop it on the floor for later disposal, or put it aside for use with a smaller sheet that will be glued. (See "scrap paper" on page 56 for suggestions on what to use.)
- When gluing a sheet of paper, start at the center and glue out to the edges, always running the brush off the edge but not back toward the center, so as not to get glue on the good underside of the sheet. I always describe this as brushing the glue on like the rays of the sun or the petals of a flower.
- When books are being pressed, line the inside covers with plastic wrap or plastic bags to provide a moisture barrier between the covers and the inside pages. This will prevent the pages from cockling (rippling).
- When stacking books to be pressed, wrap each book in waxed paper to prevent any seepage of glue from causing books to stick together.

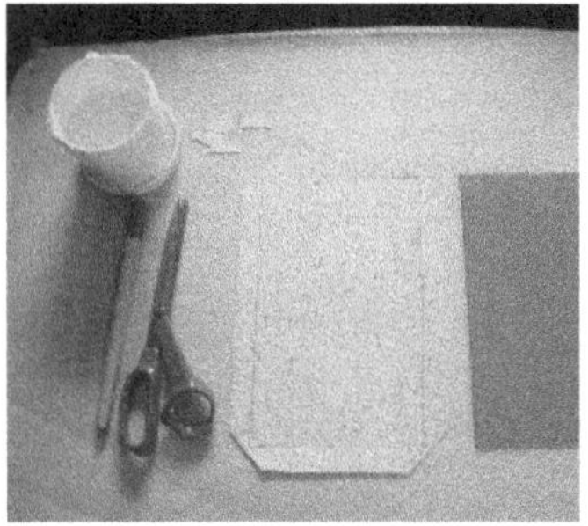
Cover paper with board traced on it and corners cut at 45 degrees.

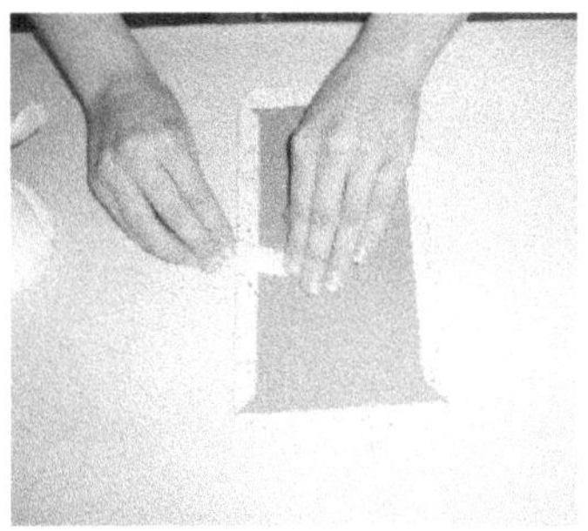
Board glued down (centered) on the cover paper, opposite sides folded in and pressed down.

Remaining sides have their corners mitered (pinched in at a diagonal over the corners of the board) and then folded and pressed down.

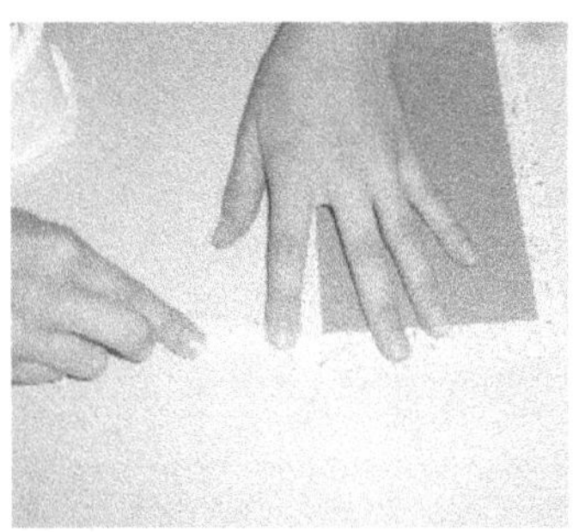
Board is covered and smoothed down with a bone folder.

Mitered Corners

Any book for which the front and back of the binding are covered boards will require mitered corners. This is the technique for trimming, folding, and gluing the cover material over the boards so that the corners are neatly tailored and not lumpy or sloppy (dwarves #8 & 9), in other words, "hospital corners" for books.

Here's how it's done:

- The covering paper is cut 1½″ larger than the board in both directions so that there's a ¾″ margin all around.
- Center the board onto the wrong side of the paper and trace around the board with a pencil. Remove the board.
- Cut the corners of the covering paper at a 45° angle, ¼″ from the corner lines that you traced in pencil.
- Coat the wrong side of the paper with glue and position the board within the lines you drew.
- Bring the top margin of the glued paper down and the opposite or bottom edge up, adhering them to the board.
- At each of the corners, make a tiny diagonal fold (as though you were wrapping a package) and fold the rest of the paper over each side of the board. You now have mitered corners. See the illustrations that show this technique.

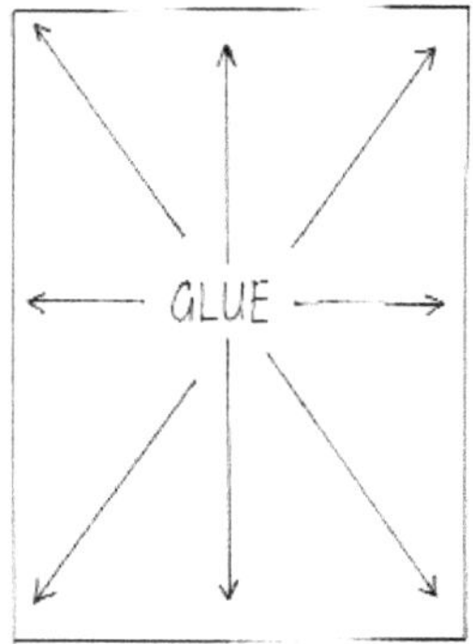

Brush glue from the center out to the edges.

Accordion Book

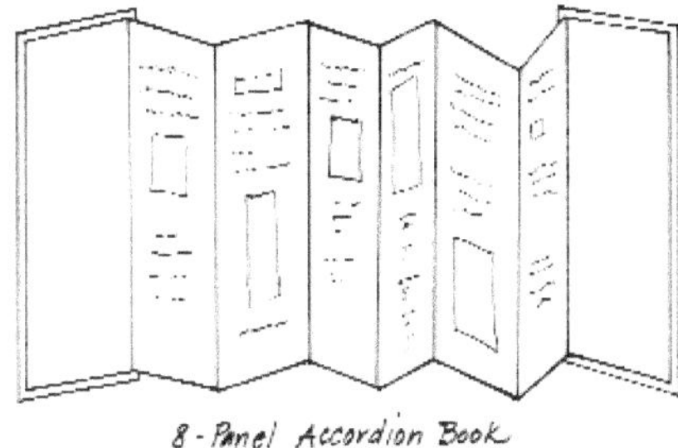

8-Panel Accordion Book

An accordion book, also called a concertina, is essentially a folded scroll with covers. The first book structure, the scroll, was one long sheet—of papyrus, parchment, paper, silk, bark—rolled up, with sections of text boxed or bracketed with lines (the first page demarcations). The folded scroll, or accordion book, offers several advantages over its predecessor:

- when closed, it is flat and compact and can sit on a shelf;
- one can leaf through pages (just as in modern book forms) rather than "scrolling" through a long continuous sheet;
- when open, it can stand on its own and every page can be seen simultaneously—the only book form with this feature;
- with such a simple structure, accordion books can be any size, from folding screen to thumbnail, and a variety of shapes; with so flexible a format, accordion books can include additional flaps, pockets, windows, and pop-ups, and still fold flat when closed.

Directions:

Materials needed for Accordion Book:

- Sheet of paper 9 × 24″ with grain parallel to 9″ side (you can get 2 books from a sheet of 18 × 24″ drawing paper)
- 2 pieces of board, each 3¼ × 9¼″
- 2 pieces of covering paper, each 4¾ × 10¾″
- Basic Bookbinding Kit

Covers:

1. Cover each board, making mitered corners, as directed above.
2. Press the boards while you are making the pages.

Text block or pages:

1. Fold the sheet of paper in half, so that it is 12 × 9″.
2. Take each end, bring it to the center, and fold so that now the piece (folded) is 6 × 9″.
3. Take each 6″ panel and fold it in half again (meeting fold to fold and smoothing down) so that your text block is now 3 × 9″.

Assembling the book:

1. Holding the accordion-folded paper flat on your hand, make a tiny "X" on the front panel, turn the whole thing over, and put a tiny "X" on the back panel.

2. Brush glue on these marked panels and adhere the front to the inside front cover and the back to the inside back cover.
3. The panel should be centered on the cover; there will be about ⅛″ of the cover showing around the text block.
4. Press the closed book under some weight until dry.

Applications and alterations to this form:

In the forthcoming section on projects, the accordion binding will be used in its most basic form (Project #2) and with alterations and additions that include pockets, extensions from an accordion spine, and sewn-in signatures (Projects #6, #7, #10, #12).

Pamphlet

The pamphlet, or what some students call "a real book," is the familiar Western form of stacked sheets, folded in half, sewn through the center crease, and enclosed in a cover that wraps around the pages. The following directions introduce two versions of the same binding: a softcover pamphlet and a hardcover pamphlet. Since one builds on the other, let's begin with the softcover.

Materials for Softcover Pamphlet:

- 5 sheets of white 8½ × 11″ paper
- 2 sheets of colored 8½ × 11″ paper
- 1 piece of cardstock or oaktag, short grain, 8¾ × 11½″
- 1 piece of decorative covering paper, 10¼ × 13″
- Basic Bookbinding Kit

Directions for Softcover Pamphlet:

1 Fold the 5 sheets of white paper in half horizontally (folded, it measures 5½ × 8½″). The sheets are folded as a group, not individually, so that they will fit together more evenly. This is your text block.

2 Fold the 2 colored sheets in half horizontally and fit these around the outside of the text block. These are your endsheets.

3. Fold the cover stock or oaktag in half horizontally and fit this around the outside of the endsheets. This is your (unfinished) cover.

4. Open the stack of folded sheets to the centerfold. Center the text block and endsheets on the inside of the cover (there will be ~⅛″ of cover showing beyond the pages) and clip the stack together (open) with clothespins. This will allow you to measure, make holes, and sew the book together without having the pages slip.

5. The pamphlet is typically a 5-hole stitch; there is a 3-hole stitch for smaller books. [see diagram] With your folio open to the centerfold, place a ruler along the length of the fold, and make a dot with a pencil in the crease at the following points along the ruler (from left to right): 1″, 2⅝″, 4¼″, 5⅞″, 7½″. These are not mysterious or arbitrary measurements; they follow the same principle for almost any size pamphlet you choose to make. The first and last stitch are positioned 1″ from either end (1″ & 7½″). The third stitch is centered on the length of the fold (4¼″). The second and fourth stitches are placed mid-point between the spaces

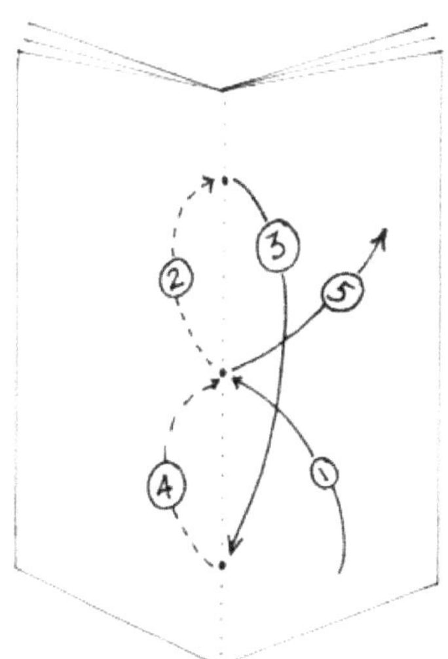

3-Hole Pamphlet Stitch

left (2 ⅝″ & 5 ⅞″). If you have a class in which ruler skills are minimal and you don't want to waste a lot of time trying to explain which line is the eighth inch, photocopy the template on page 152 and distribute to your students.

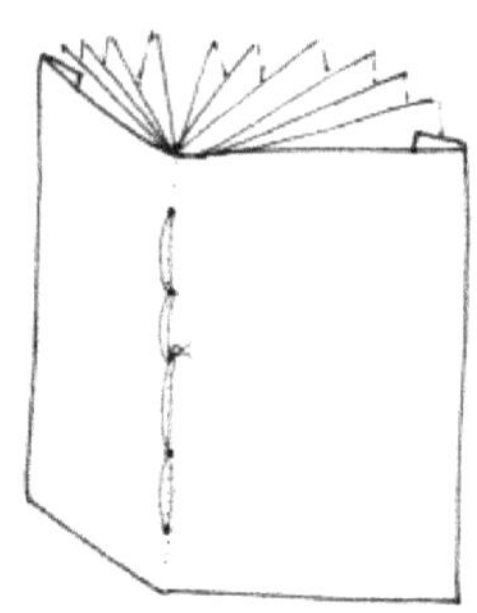

Simple softcover pamphlet with 5-hole stitch

6. Once these marks are made, pierce holes through all the layers of the centerfold with an awl. Make sure the awl enters in the crease and emerges outside on the spine fold (not to the right or left of it).
7. Take a piece of thread about 18 – 20″ long, rub the length of it through the beeswax 2 or 3 times, and thread the needle. You will be sewing with a single thread. Do not make a knot at the end of the thread.
8. Follow the order of stitches indicated on the illustration. For the pamphlet stitch, wherever you start is where you'll finish. In other words, we will sew the first stitch going from the outside spine into the inside centerfold, and will make the final stitch and knot the thread on the outside spine. This also means that if you want the ending knot to show on the inside of the book, you can start the first stitch on the inside and that's where you'll end up.

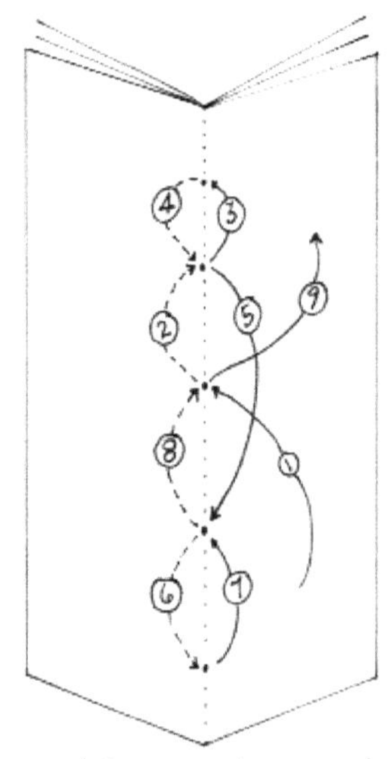

5-hole pamphlet stitch (see template on page 153 for a larger view and detailed instructions)

9. Once the final stitch is made, knot the two ends of the thread over the central long stitch, and clip the ends with a scissors, leaving ¼″ of thread (i.e. don't clip right down to the knot).
10. Remove the clothespins.
11. If you don't want to cover the oaktag, or have used a heavyweight decorative coverstock, you can stop here and consider your simple softcover pamphlet complete. To cover the oaktag, keep reading.

12. Fold the covering paper horizontally and place wrong side up. 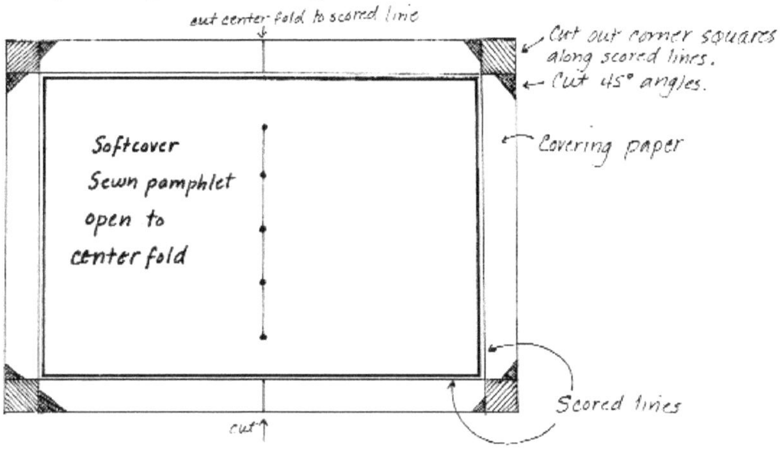
13. Open the sewn pamphlet to the centerfold and center it on the covering paper. There will be a ¾″ margin of paper showing around the outside dimensions of the book. With a pencil, trace around the cover of the book on the wrong side of the cover paper.
14. Remove the book.
15. Extend the lines you've drawn out to the edges of the cover paper. You will have ¾″ squares in each corner.
16. Place a ruler directly on each of the lines you've drawn and score with a bone folder. The thickness of the bone folder will insure that the scored lines are just outside the actual dimensions of the book, which will allow the paper to fit around the cover.
17. At each corner, cut out the square along the scored lines (not the drawn lines; you need a tiny bit extra to hide the cardstock). Clip the corners at a 45° angle (see diagram). When this is glued down, it will resemble a mitered corner.
18. At the centerfold of the cover paper, cut 2 slits from the edge of the paper to the lines you drew indicating the top and the bottom of the book.
19. Since this is a lot of paper to glue all at once, we'll do it half at a time. Place the cover paper wrong side up on a larger piece of scrap paper. Place the sewn book, closed, on the cover paper, with the spine aligned to the centerfold and fitting within the top and bottom lines. Half of your cover paper is exposed.
20. Brush glue on this half.
21. Open just the cover of the sewn book onto the glued surface and smooth down. Fold the top and bottom flaps of cover paper over the cover and smooth down. Fold the out-

side (fore edge) flap into the cover and smooth down. Do the same thing for the other half of the book.

22. The final step is to glue down one of the endsheets onto the inside front and back covers. Place a piece of scrap paper between the first and second endsheets*, and brush glue onto the surface that's facing the inside cover. Close the cover onto the glued sheet (helps with alignment) and smooth out any air bubbles or wrinkles with your bone folder.
23. Place plastic wrap around the text block, close the book, and place under some weight to press until dry.

Materials for Hardcover Pamphlet:

- 5 sheets of white 8½ × 11″ paper
- 2 sheets of colored 8½ × 11″ paper
- 1 piece of cardstock or oaktag, 3 × 8½″
- 1 piece of bookcloth, 3 × 10″
- 2 pieces of matboard, 5¼ × 8½″
- 2 pieces of decorative covering paper, 5 × 10″
- Basic Bookbinding Kit

Directions for Hardcover Pamphlet:

1. The hardcover pamphlet is similar to the softcover described above. Start by folding the white and colored sheets as before.
2. Take the narrow strip of cardstock and fold in half vertically (it will be 1½ × 8½″). Fit this around the outside of the folded textblock and endsheets, open to the center fold, and clip together with clothespins. This narrow strip is your cover hinge.
3. Measure along the centerfold, mark and pierce holes as before.
4. Sew the book together, as before, starting on the outside (spine) edge.
5. Remove the clothespins.
6. On each side of the hinge, draw a line down the length of the hinge, ¼″ from the

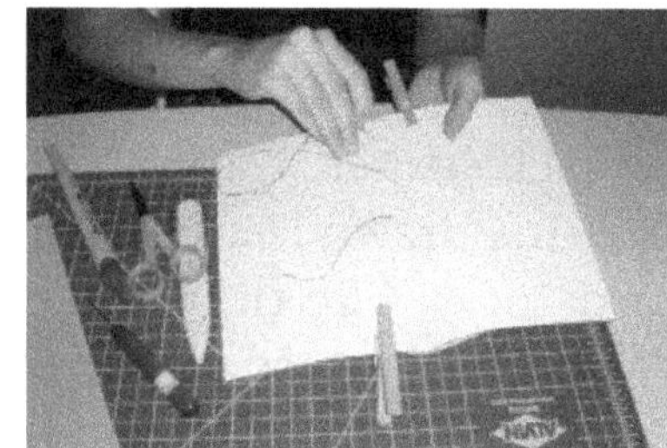

Step 2: Pamphlet is sewn; the pages, end papers, and cardstock hinge are secured with clothes pins.

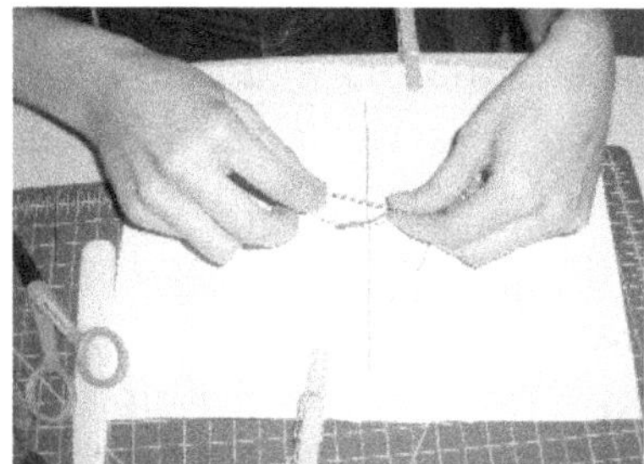

Step 4: Pamphlet stitch is finished with a knot.

Hardcover pamphlet

* It's traditional to have two endsheets. The one glued to the inside cover is the "pastedown" and the one that is "free" is the "flyleaf."

spine edge. Place a piece of scrap paper between the hinge and the endsheets, and brush glue from the line out to the edge of the hinge.

7. Align one piece of matboard with the drawn line and adhere it to the hinge. Do the same for the other cover.
8. Fold the length of bookcloth vertically (soft fold, not sharp crease) and mark on the wrong side where this center line is (see illustration at right). If you are using dark bookcloth, use a white or yellow colored pencil so that your marks will show. Measure up ¾″ from either short edge of the bookcloth and draw a line on the wrong side. You now have marks that will help you to place the book centered on the bookcloth and with equal overhang top and bottom.
9. Brush glue onto the wrong side of the bookcloth. Place the book, open to the centerfold, onto the glued surface of the bookcloth.
10. Gently lift the sewn pages and endsheets, first at the top and fold the bookcloth over, adhering it to the hinge and cover. Repeat at the bottom.
11. Close the book and smooth the bookcloth into the ridges where the front and back boards meet the hinge (the French groove).

Step 6: Outside of sewn pamphlet with lines drawn on the hinge to show placement of cover boards.

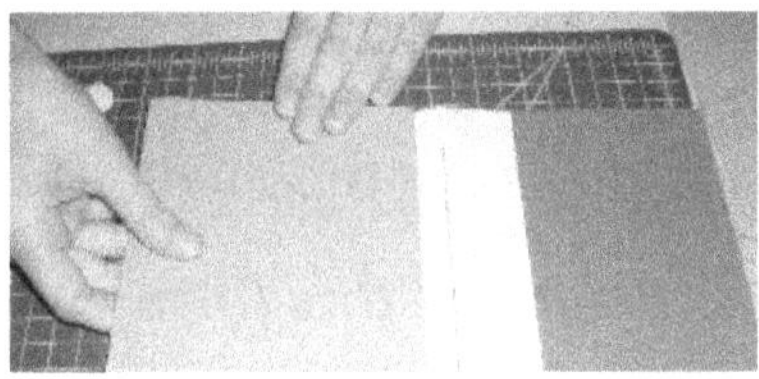

Step 6 (cont'd): Paste is applied to the hinge and each board is placed on the line.

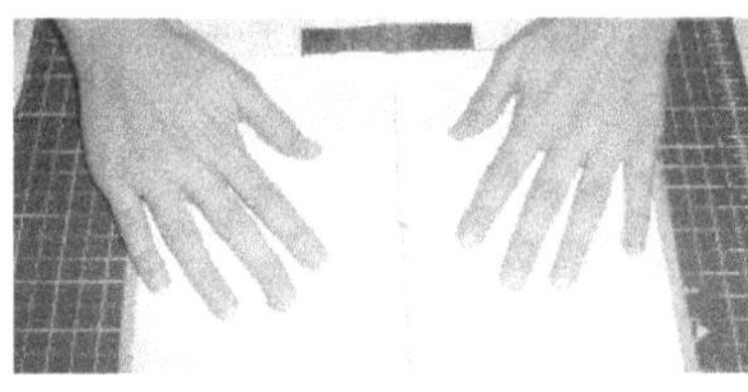

Step 9: After paste has been applied to the book cloth, the pamphlet is placed on it, aligning the center fold with the center line and the bottom with the marked margin.

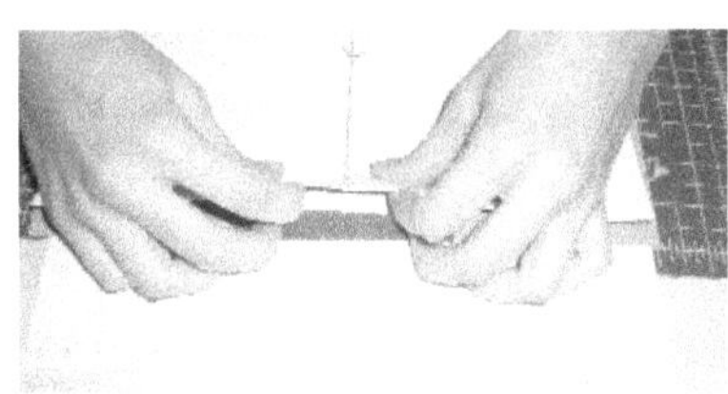

Step 10: Text block (pages and end papers) are lifted to allow the book cloth to be tucked over and adhered to the hinge, top and bottom.

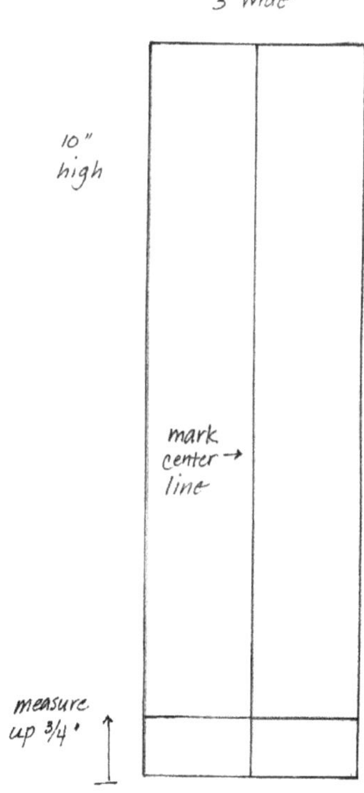

Step 8: Marking bookcloth (*wrong side*) for hardcover pamphlet

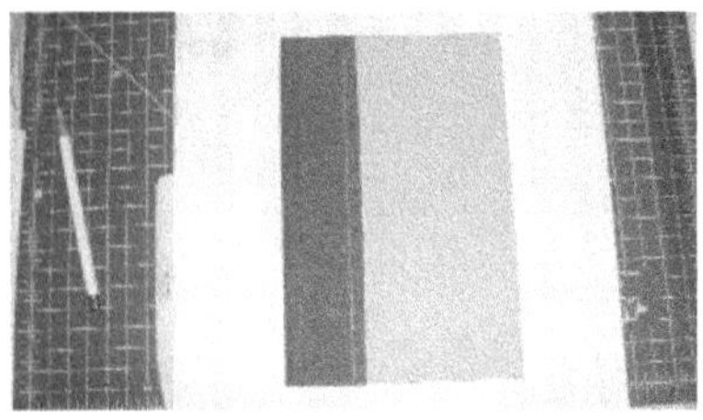

Steps 11 & 12: Hardcover pamphlet closed, showing the French groove scored and a line drawn 1/4" in from the edge of the book cloth (front and back) for the alignment of the covering paper.

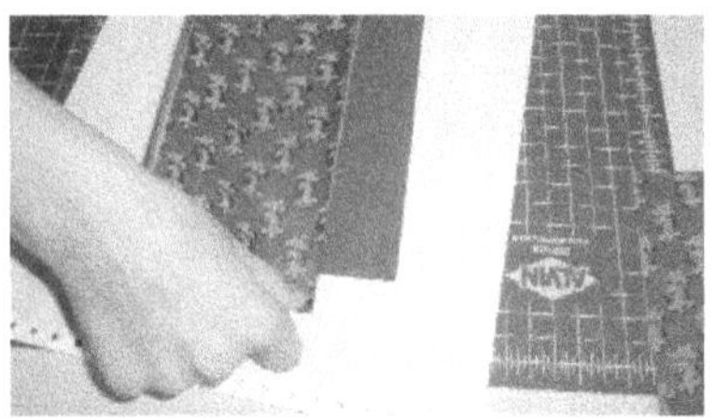

Step 13: Covering paper is glued, placed on the line, and smoothed down.

Step 13 (cont'd): Outer corners are cut at a 45 degree angle, folded, mitered, and pressed down.

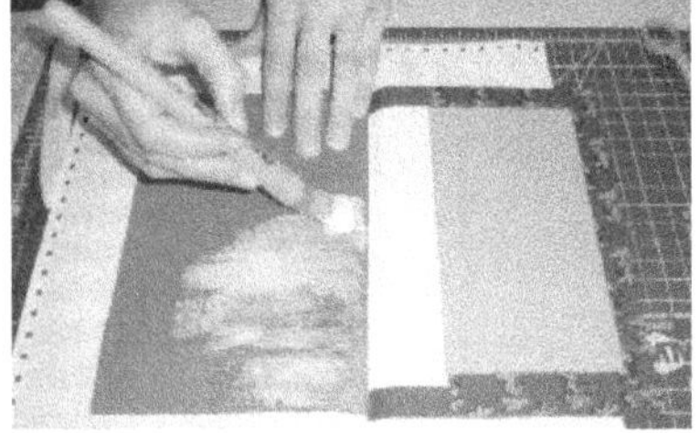

Step 14: First endsheet is glued, after which the cover will be closed onto it (to prevent air bubbles) and then opened to smooth down any ripples. Once the front and back covers are adhered to the endsheets, the book is finished and ready to be pressed until dry.

12. Measure in 1¼″ from the spine and draw a light line on the bookcloth, front and back covers. This is where you will align the covering paper.
13. Place a sheet of covering paper wrong side up and brush with glue. Place the glued surface onto a cover of the book, lined up with the line you just drew on the bookcloth. Trim the two corners at a 45° angle, and finish covering the board with mitered corners. Repeat for the other cover.
14. The last step is to adhere the pastedown endsheets to the inside front and back covers. This is done the same way as for the softcover pamphlet. Insert plastic moisture barriers and press the finished book under some weight until dry.

Applications of this form:

In the forthcoming section on projects, the pamphlet will be used in its hardcover version for project #3, as a softcover form in projects #4 & 5, and as a springboard either in hard or softcover for project #12.

Stab-Bound Book

Post & screw

As with the pamphlet, the stab-bound book can be made in softcover or hardcover versions; both will be described. This ancient Asian form developed from a need to bind accordion volumes more securely along one edge. The accordion book, without hardcover, was stabbed through with a line of holes along one edge, and then laced together with cords. Over time, the stitching of the binding became an art in itself, with many elaborate variations. One basic stab-bound stitch will be shown here; a good source of instruction for more decorative stitches is listed below.[1]

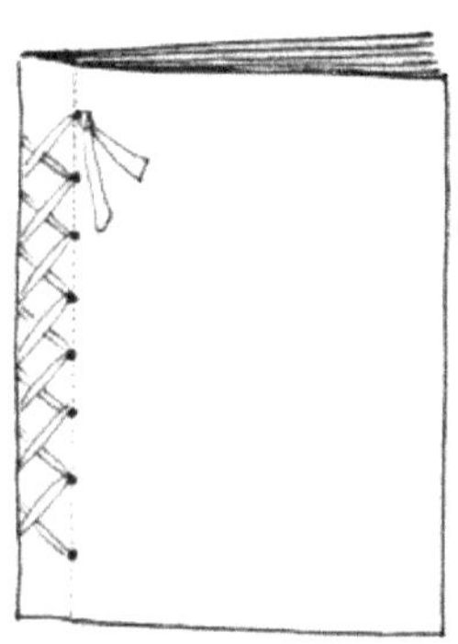

Criss-cross stitch

Stab-bound books are often called albums in the West, because they are put together in the same way photo albums and scrapbooks often appear: separate sheets between two covers through which holes are punched and attachments added. Both versions of the stab-binding described here will use stitching, but easy alternatives abound for those who don't want to be bothered with the complicated sewing of this form. Fasteners called "posts & screws" which are often used in albums can be purchased at some stationery stores, arts and crafts stores that cater to scrapbooking, and through mail order. Holes can be punched through the covers and pages and, instead of sewing, a thin ribbon can be laced through, even criss-crossed and tied with a bow. This type of binding is often seen on more decorative albums for weddings, baby memorabilia, and other special occasions. Finally, a very simple attachment can be made by punching just two holes through the cover and pages, inserting an elastic band from the back through the holes, and holding it in place with a stick, pencil, dowel, large nail, chopstick, etc.

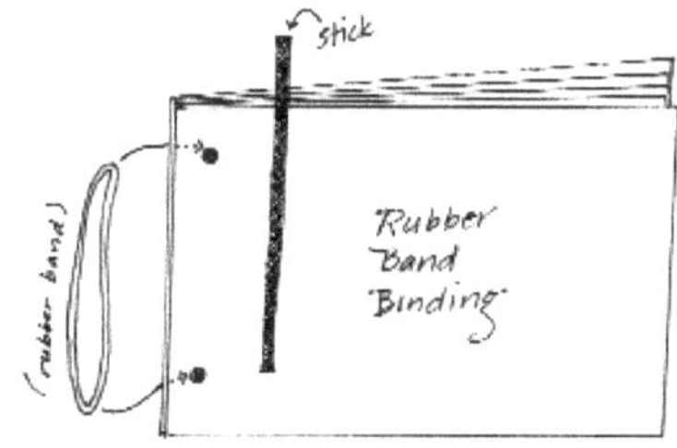

Insert each end of rubber band through hole from the back. Insert stick through rubberband loops that emerge from the holes.

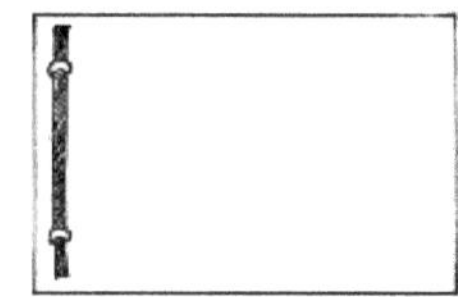

[1] *Japanese Bookbinding: Instructions from a Master Craftsman*, by Kojiro Ikegami. NY: Weatherhill, 1986.

Materials needed for the Softcover stab binding:

- 10 sheets of paper, 8 ½× 11″
- 2 sheets of coverstock or heavy decorative paper, 8½× 5½″
- Basic Bookbinding Kit, minus the glue
- about 1 yard of waxed thread *
- optional: beads or charms to decorate the ends of binding strings

* Measuring out the correct amount of thread sometimes is tricky. Here's a rule of thumb for this book form: multiply the height of the book (in this case, 5½″) by the number of sewing holes (5). This gives you 27½″ of thread, which is sufficient for sewing with a single thread, knotting and having a bit left over on which one could attach a bead or charm. If you want to sew the book with a double thread, which looks nicer, double the sum (27½″x 2 = 55″).

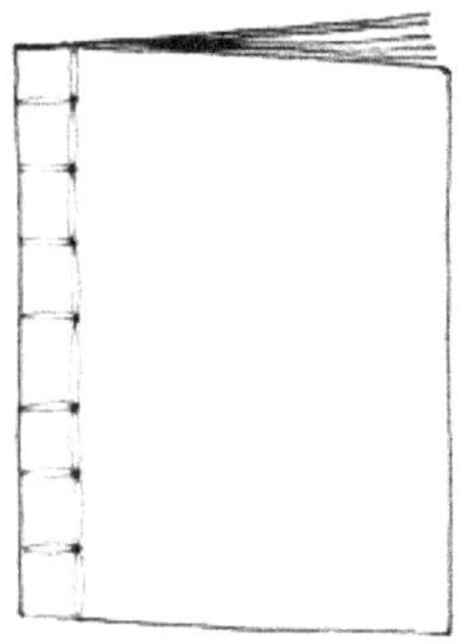

stab · bound stitch

Directions for the S*OFTCOVER* *stab binding:*

1. Cut all 10 sheets of paper in half horizontally, so that each student has 20 sheets of paper, 8½× 5½″.
2. Put a cover on the top and bottom of the stack of pages and clip the pile together with clothespins.
3. This is a horizontal format, so the spine is 5½″ high. From the spine edge, measure and mark ½″ in, and draw a faint line on the top cover. This line will be covered by stitching.
4. Hold a ruler along this line, and make a dot on the line at the following points: ¾″, 1¾″, 2¾″, 3¾″, 4¾″. (In other words, ¾″ in from the top and bottom edge, and the rest of the holes are placed 1″ apart.) We will use 5 holes for this binding, but any number—3 or more—can be used. (Hint: Perhaps a particular number would fit in with your theme; plan on using that number of holes for this binding.)
5. I'll describe the stitching, but it may be easier to follow from the diagram. Starting at the bottom hole on the back of the book, insert threaded needle into the hole, out the front of the book, into the next hole up, out the back of the book, and so on in a running stitch until you get through the last hole at the top. Wrap the thread around the top of the book and back through the same hole you just left. Now wrap the thread around the spine edge of the book and back into the hole you just left. Insert the needle through the next hole down, emerge from the cover, and wrap the thread around the spine edge and back into that hole again. Repeat the directions in this last sentence until you get to the bottom of the book. At that point, wrap the thread around the bottom, but instead of going into the last hole, slip the needle under the previous stitches around this hole and knot the remaining thread with the tail left from the first stitch.
6. If you'd rather not have the ending knot on the back of the book, start at the top hole in the front cover and proceed the same way. You can string beads, charms, etc. on the hanging strings, or you can tie them or braid them into a tassel and trim neatly. Wherever you start stitching this book is where you'll end up.

Directions for the HARDCOVER *stab binding:*

The two pieces that form each cover of the album connect with a hinge of bookcloth that allows the cover to open flat and a full view of each page. The first directions are for constructing the cover. Then I'll describe a way to customize album pages that will permit mounting photos or other collaged items. Assembling—or sewing the pages into the cover—follows the same procedure as for the softcover stab bound book.

1. On the wrong side of each larger piece of bookcloth, measure in from either long side 1¾″ and 2″. Draw two parallel vertical lines at these measurements. (See illustration at right)
2. At the bottom of the bookcloth, measure up ¾″ from one of the short sides, mark it and draw a horizontal line.
3. These marks indicate placement of the cover boards. If you are using black or dark bookcloth, a white or yellow pencil comes in handy. The 1″ wide piece of board will be aligned with the line drawn at 1¾″. The larger piece of cover board will be aligned with the line drawn at 2″ There will be a ¼″ gap between the two boards which will serve as a hinge.
4. Brush glue on the smaller piece of board and align it with the vertical and horizontal lines drawn on the bookcloth.
5. Brush glue on the rest of the bookcloth and place the larger board in its place.

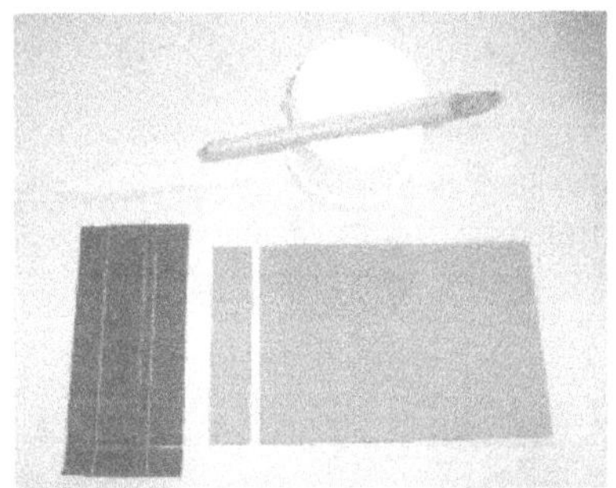

Step 4: Materials for constructing a hardcover stab-bound binding: book cloth marked with lines for aligning the boards; two boards, the hinge and the cover; glue and glue brush.

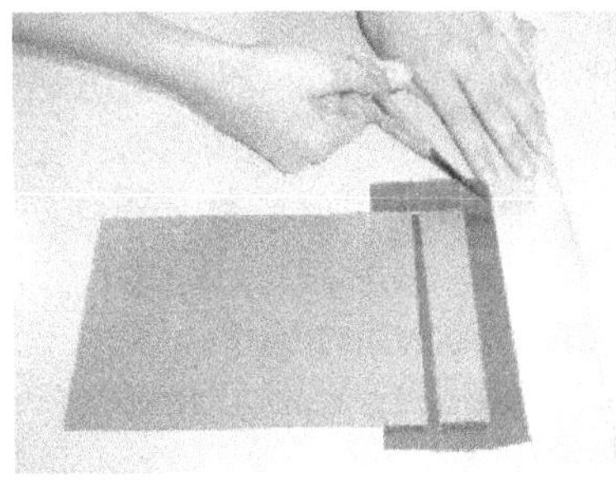

Step 5: Boards pasted and placed on the marked book cloth.

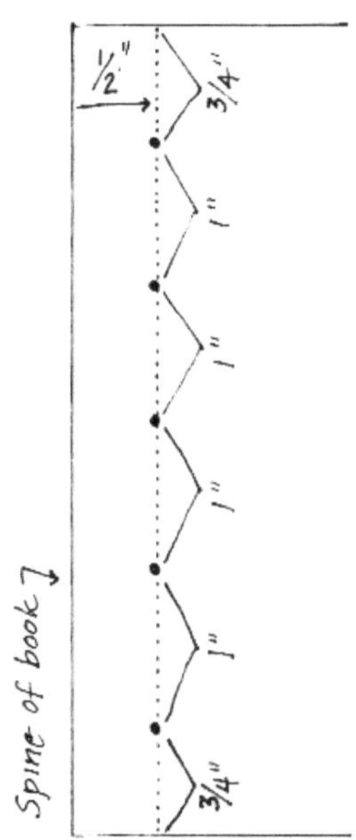

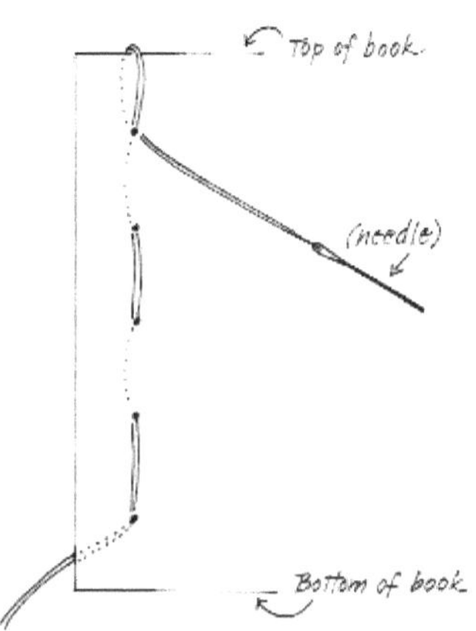

Materials needed for the Hardcover stab binding:

- 2 boards, 9×11″
- 2 boards, 9×1″
- 2 pieces of bookcloth, 3×10½″
- 2 pieces of bookcloth, 2¼×8¾″
- 2 pieces covering paper, 11×10½″
- 2 pieces covering paper, 9¾×8¾″
- paper for pages, 8¾×12″ (cut down from 9×12″)
- Basic Bookbinding Kit
- optional: ¹⁄₁₆″ hole punch

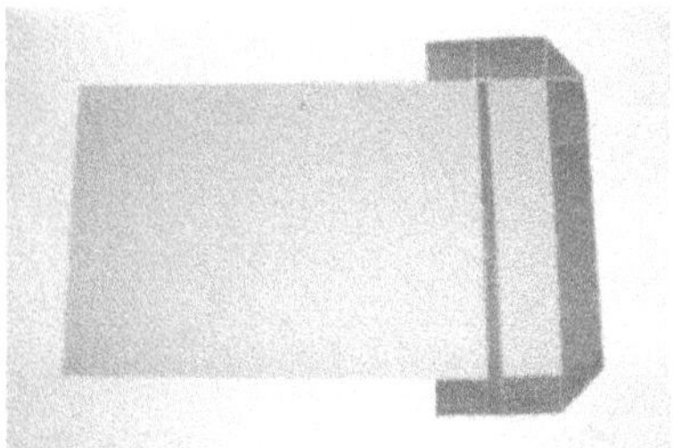

Step 6: Two outer corners cut at 45 degree angles.

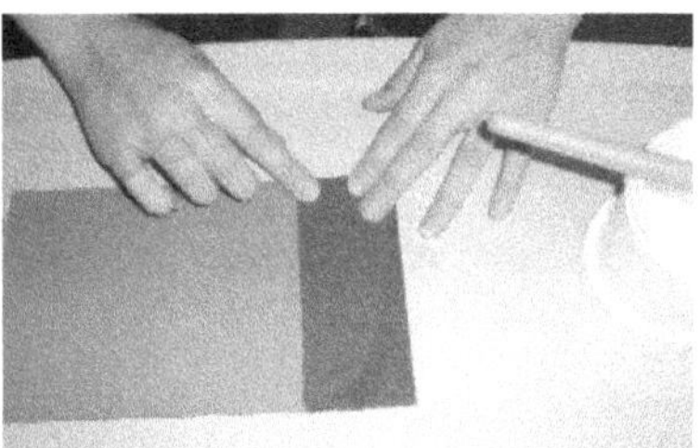

Step 8: Glue the bookcloth liner in place on the inside of the cover.

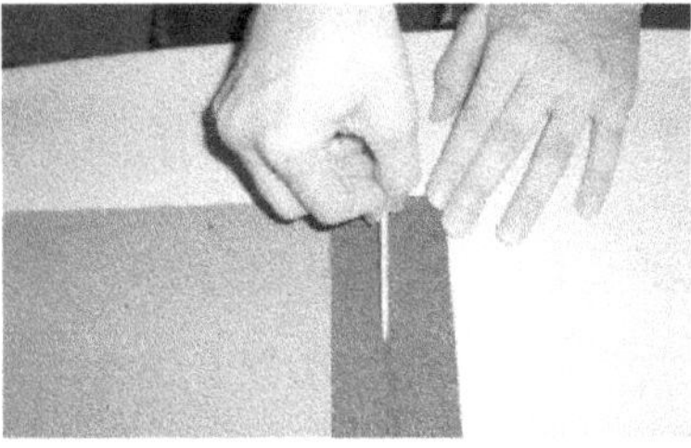

Step 8 (cont'd): Cloth hinge (top and bottom layers of book cloth) pressed and smoothed with bone folder.

6. While the glue is still wet, diagonally cut the outer corners at the top and bottom of the bookcloth, along the edge where the narrow board is adhered. (See page 62 for instructions on making mitered corners.)
7. Proceed to fold the top and bottom edges of bookcloth over the boards, miter the outer corners, and fold over the side edge. Repeat the same with the other cover.

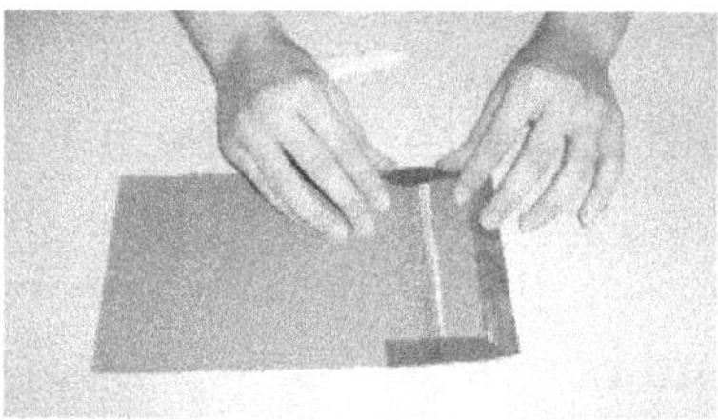

Step 7: Remaining cloth is pasted, the corners mitered, and the edges folded over and smoothed down.

8. Brush glue on the wrong side of the bookcloth liner and adhere it to the inside of each cover.
9. Where the edge of the bookcloth ends on the larger cover board, measure in ¼″ and draw a faint line. Do this for both the front and back covers.

Step 9: Book cloth is marked, 1/4" in from edge, for the alignment of the cover paper.

10. Glue up the cover paper (one piece at a time); align it with the faint line you just drew on the bookcloth; cut the outer corners of the cover paper, fold down the top and bottom edges, miter the corners, and fold in the fore edge.
11. Paste in the liner for the cover and repeat with the other cover.

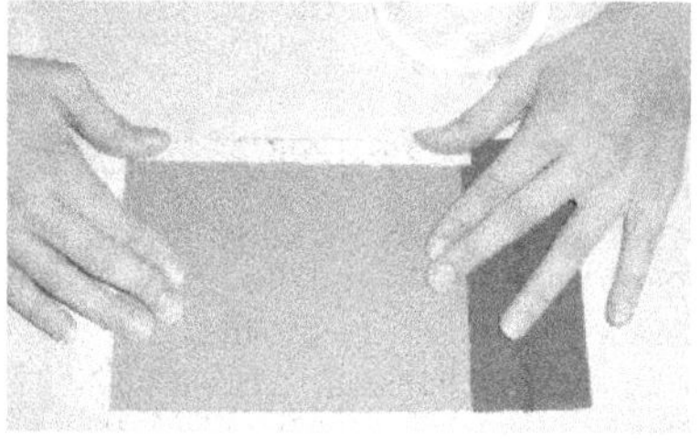

Steps 10 & 11: Cover paper is glued, lined up to the mark on the cloth, folded over, mitered and pressed. Inside cover is lined with matching cover paper.

12. If pages are to be sewn into these album covers, punch holes through the boards. Using the holes in the front cover board as the template, mark the placement of holes on the pages and then punch. It's advisable to use a heavier thread and to double it when sewing a hardcover stab-binding. Proceed with the same sewing pattern described for the softcover stab-bound book.

13. If, instead of sewing the binding, you'd prefer to use post & screws, small bolts and nuts, ribbon, hinged rings, or a stick and rubberband binding, you will need to drill only 2 holes through the covers and pages.
14. A few finishing touches: If your pages are a heavy paper or cardstock, they will turn more easily if you score them 1½″ from the bound edge. This would need to be done before the book is assembled. If you plan to mount photos or additional sheets on the pages (i.e. if you are using this book as an album or scrapbook rather than as a book just to write in), you should add spacers to the binding. A simple way to do this is to take 1″ strips of the same paper used for the pages and neatly adhere these strips on the page along the edge that will be hidden under the binding. Glue stick works for this. Then, when you pierce holes for sewing or binding, you will include the spacer. Spacers will thicken up the spine, which allows the book to lie flat once it is filled instead of fanning open at the fore edge.

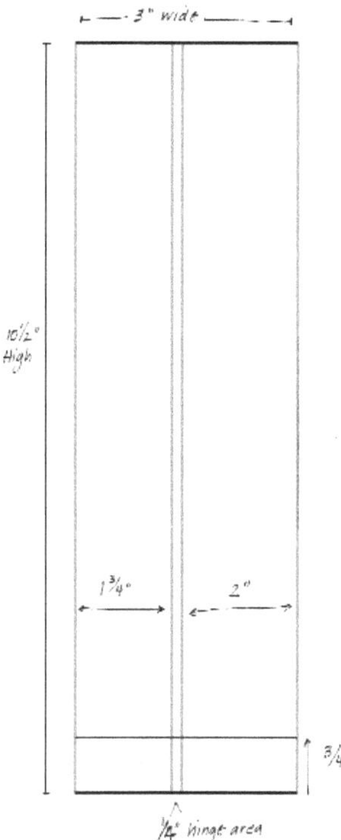

Marking bookcloth (*wrong side*) for hardcover stab binding

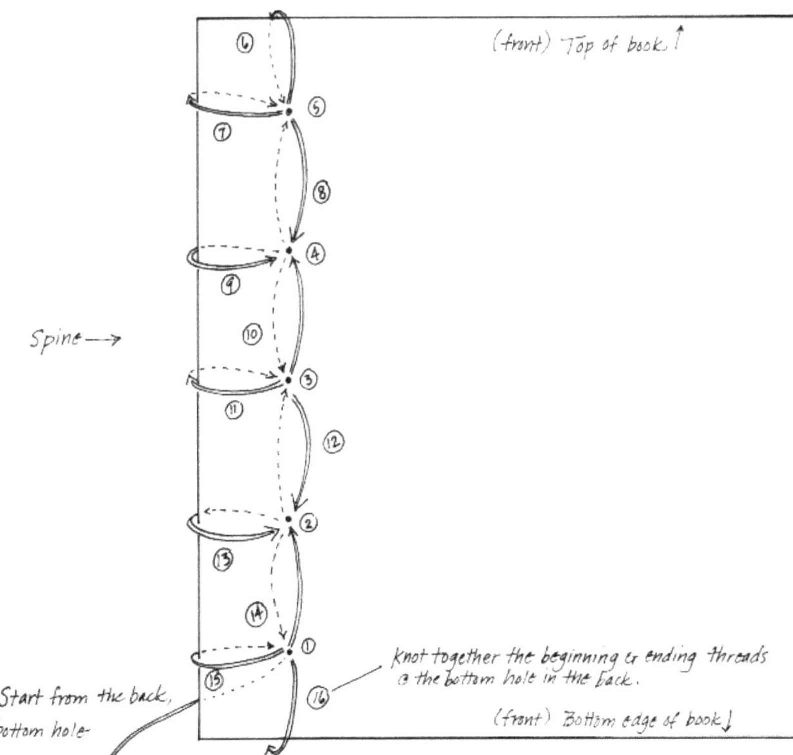

Applications of this form:

In the forthcoming section on projects, the simplest form of stab-bound book will be used for project #1. Project #9 will use the hardcover form of this binding in exactly the same size as described here.

7 Revision and Evaluation

Critiquing and grading are especially challenging with regard to highly subjective and individualized creative work. There are ways, however, to instruct and improve with encouragement and to assess progress and accomplishment without a dart board!

Revision: The Art of Seeing All Over Again

Most of today's students learn to take their writing through a series of steps, a writing process, before they consider an essay or story finished. Students learn to brainstorm (generate ideas), draft (get the ideas on paper), rewrite with form or content in mind (cut, expand, shift words), and then polish (edit grammar, find spelling mistakes). Poetry is written much the same way. The warm-up activities before a writing session might be considered the brainstorming stage or prewriting of the poem. A poem is drafted, the ideas captured onto the paper. Then the poem needs to be revised.

"Revision is the act of becoming one's own teacher."

Poets develop personal and idiosyncratic work habits when it comes to both generating and revising poems. Some poets revise very little; others revise exhaustively. The process of revision can be a walk along a high wire: "It's often hard to capture the delicate mood and flow you had while writing the first draft," the poet and educator Jack Collom reminds us.[1] Sometimes poets find it helpful to let a poem sit for a period of time before attempting to revisit it. Difficulties

[1] Jack Collom, *Poetry Everywhere*, p. 241

notwithstanding, poems usually benefit from revision if revision is approached as an opportunity not to correct but to re-see the work.

I like to start a lesson on revision by writing "RE VISION" up on a blackboard and asking the students what each piece of the word, thus divided, means. "Vision" involves seeing or perceiving. The prefix "Re" connotes a repetition or doing again. Hence revision for a poet involves the process of looking anew at the material or reentering the scene or mood created. It is helpful to distinguish this process from copy-editing, or proofing and correcting, which may involve grammar, punctuation, and syllable counts. A poet will want to consider all of these elements of language usage as part of his/her revision process, but revision itself also involves letting the mind range in a larger field. "Revision," says Collom, "is the act of becoming one's own teacher."[2] The poet approaches her own piece much as if she is considering the work of another class member. The poet interrogates her own poem.

RE VISION

The questions on the facing page help guide students through this interrogation process and may be useful as well when students are learning to give feedback to other student poets.

It is important for students to know that they are the ultimate judges when it comes to their own poems. I encourage students to keep original drafts and subsequent drafts. I often cut and paste pieces from different versions of a poem in order to create a final form. Sometimes I show students several drafts of a piece of my own writing. It may be useful to try out a variation in a poem if only to discover that you as the poet do not like the change and that the original more precisely or more musically says what you want to say. Encourage a sense of play in the revision process; students can always reclaim their original drafts.

---

[2] Jack Collom, *Poetry Everywhere*, p. 241

Some Questions to Ask When Revising or Giving Feedback on Creative Writing

- What is the central idea in this piece of writing?
- What emotion, if any, do the words arouse in you, the reader?
- What words or phrases stand out as particularly effective?
- Where is the work's primary energy? Where is it most vivid or visual? Where does the poem start for you?
- Do tone/ rhythm/ rhyme scheme/ music match the material in the poem, the content and feeling?
- Are there words or images that could be more precise?
- Does the language shift between formal and informal or conversational? Are the shifts deliberate? Effective?
- Are some images obscure? Is the obscurity lending the work a desired sense of mystery? Are some images so obscure they're just confusing and thus kicking the reader out of the poem?
- Is punctuation positive or distracting in any way? (There are no firm rules for punctuating a poem but the writer should know why he or she employs punctuation or not, uses capital letters or does not.)
- Is the point of view consistent? If not, where are shifts in point of view made? Do the shifts work? If the point of view stays consistent, is consistency your most effective tool for this work?
- How does the form on the page fit the mood of the work? How does the form on the page fit the message?
- Read your poem out loud to yourself, your cat, your friend or your wall. Does the sound of the work fit the content or mood of the piece?

Sometimes it is helpful to remind students of the way good "come-back lines" form. Maybe they will have had a fight with a friend or parent. It may take the whole day of rethinking the argument to realize what they "should have said." Revision ideas may come to students after a poem has simmered for a while as well.

The degree to which a student will be able or willing to revise will clearly vary with the age, level of sophistication, and writing level of the individual. Teachers can help even the most reluctant writer to reenter his or her work with a few gentle nudges.

- Ask the student to read the poem aloud to you.
- Read it aloud again back to the student.
- Have students shut their eyes and re-imagine their poems. Try adding details. Use all five senses: sight, sound, scent, texture, taste.
- Don't forget other details that can enhance a piece: weather, specific numbers, proper nouns.
- Encourage students to reexamine nouns and verbs. Instead of just saying "tree," could you name the type? How did the dog move across the floor? Would "sidled" give more of a picture than "walked," for example?
- Suggest that students consult a thesaurus. Find synonyms for overused or less interesting words. Find alternatives to words that do not enhance the rhythm of a work.
- Try varying the look of the piece on the page. Break lines in new places. (Computers are great for this stage. Just keep drafts and versions.) Print out the piece with variations in line breaks or changes in lines per stanza and see, literally, what looks best for this poem.
- Suggest that students work with a "revision buddy." Have students respond to one another's work using the questions above as a starting place for their evaluations.

A Word About Revision and the Artist Book

The first step in making any type of artist book is to make a "quick & dirty" model, using scrap paper that is cut to size and the most rudimentary binding (e.g. a stapler). If windows, pockets, or flaps are envisioned, they can be taped onto the model pages. Text can be written out on Post-it® notes and moved around in the model book to help determine the number of pages needed. Before any "good" materials are used, a physical model can be rapidly revised.

"Make a 'quick and dirty' model with scrap paper, stapler, tape, and Post-it® notes before any 'good' materials are used."

For a project that originates with text, the form of the model will need to reflect the theme and mood of the writing. Projects that begin with the book form can freely experiment with dimensions, binding, and inclusions (doors, flaps, pockets, etc.) to create an environment to which text will respond.

Once a form is finalized, meaning that the size, shape, and number of pages have been determined, the many other visual and verbal choices will be made by the individual artist and will help dictate the next step.

When students are incorporating words into their books, they may want to reshape the writing to fit the form of the individual page on which it will appear. Tracing paper is a handy tool for seeing how writing looks on the physical environment of the particular page. Treated Mylar® is even better, but more expensive. Students can write their text onto translucent paper or acetate and literally move words around on the page to see if a particular layout of the language works with the visual stage provided on each page. Another useful tool is a photocopy machine, especially a color copier. For timid artists who don't want to "mess up" their surfaced papers, a few trials on copies of the real thing can defuse their anxiety.

When revising writing, the artist can change his mind without losing the original or altered versions. When revising a piece of visual art, however, the artist risks destroying a piece of, for example, marbled paper by changing his mind about size, type, or placement of text or images. It's a good idea to continually remind students that "It's only paper!" At this point in their development, they shouldn't be forming extreme attachments to works in progress—even mature artists need to cultivate the courage to experiment, revise, and possibly ruin a piece in search of the best aesthetic solutions.

Evaluation of Student Work

Textbooks on the subject of teaching poetry in schools often advise against subjecting student work to evaluation and assessment standards. There are obvious problems with this advice. Most teachers need to present some assessment of student work to their administrations, to the students' parents, and to the student. Practically speaking, most teachers will need to devise some way of determining whether a student has succeeded in completing his/her artist book project to an acceptable, or higher, degree.

Beyond this need to respond to administrative requirement, however, a teacher honors a student work by holding it to some standard of evaluation. When a teacher offers a critical (and by this we mean not negatively criticizing but critiquing) response to what a student presents as finished work, the teacher allows the student to learn that the making of poetry and of books involves sets of real skills. These are skills that can not only be mastered, but refined. Joseph Tsujimoto notes that often "Poetry...is deemed...a divine gift"[3] and that, consequently, "according to some students, some parents, and even some teachers criticizing a student's poem is tantamount to sacrilege." Tsujimoto and other arts educators see this assumption as having the unfortunate effect of dissuading some teachers from advising, instructing and evaluating student work. Students can and will learn from teacher response.

Initially, most teachers will find student poetry lacking in "sustained versification skill, precision of thought, conscious subtlety, or breadth of metaphoric reference."[4] However, there are qualities we can expect even in young children's poetry. These, according to Collom, include:

- Candidness
- Energy
- Sound sense and rhythm
- The ability to show and not tell a scene with specific detail

---

[3] Joseph I.Tsujimoto, *Teaching Poetry Writing to Adolescents*, p. 25
[4] Jack Collom, *Moving Windows*, p. ix

- Some use of surrealism (images from dream) and metaphor
- Concision and understatement, or what Collom refers to as "shortening, shaping and shutting up."[5]

The list of questions a student might use in revision provides a teacher with a useful guide for evaluating the finished product of students. (See page 79, *Some Questions to Ask*)

You might initiate the evaluation process by holding an individual conference with the student; sit with the student and review the work in the context of these questions. Where you see room for growth in a particular area (e.g., rhythm or sound sense in the poem), do offer advice. Tsujimoto believes in giving the student as much advice as the teacher can. "What I mean by advice is for the teacher to suggest changes; to offer alternative words and means, asking the student to compare them with what the student has written; to ask the student to expand or compress, deepen or extend thoughts and feelings—that is, the teacher does exactly what student revisers do."[6] Do keep in mind that the word of a teacher carries a great deal of weight; beware the delicate ego of the student artist. Try to keep your feedback focused on the positive. Find some place where a student made a good move—a sharp word choice, a great line break, a particularly neatly mitered corner—and then point out where this skill can be used to improve the work in another place in the writing or book form.

If a grade is to be assigned to a project, it is useful to create (in advance of assigning the project) a limited set of rubrics by which the final piece will be evaluated and to inform students by what standards projects will be graded. Try to be specific in this list of objectives. For example, you may ask if original figures of speech are used, or if cliches fill the writing. Does word placement on the page demonstrate that an attempt was made to match form to message or are the words laid out in a totally random, or totally formulaic manner? Were the choices regarding materials, techniques, colors, style of writing, etc. supportive of the theme of the text? Each project can be

What might a teacher look for in students' artist books? When evaluating their work, we pose these questions:

- Does the student's poem or book represent either a new or original piece, or a classic story retold in a fresh way?
- Does it flow and keep our attention?
- How well is the piece executed technically? (writing skills, bookmaking skills)
- Do the form and content support each other?

[5] Jack Collom, *Moving Windows*, p. x
[6] Joseph I.Tsujimoto, *Teaching Poetry Writing to Adolescents*, p. 27

assessed by a particular and defined set of standards. Other issues can be noted but not included in the tallying of the final grade.

For each of the projects on the following pages, teachers should require students to write an artist statement. Students need to articulate what they've done and why. This will help you to assess their progress. An artist's statement describes the intent of the project, why certain choices were made, and how the form and content support each other.

Students need to articulate what they've done and why.

In evaluating students' competence as book artists, teachers must keep in mind that some students will be better or worse at making things with their hands. We believe an honest attempt at following directions and creating the book form should be rewarded. Evaluation should not solely hinge on the finished product, but also on sincerely trying to complete the process. Students who make many books will make better and better books.

In his book *Free Play*, Stephen Nachmanovitch notes that all artists are able to make some good or even great art only by making a lot of art. Happy accidents occur when creative risks are taken. New skills are developed only when new processes are tried. Evaluation standards that encourage investment in process and not just pride in a particular individual project will, over time, embolden students to take creative risks and thus strengthen creative thinking skills. These are the very skills we seek to enhance when we ask students to enter the world of the book artist.

If you are interested in reading a thorough discussion of evaluation of student creative writing, we highly recommend Jack Collum's book *Moving Windows: Evaluating the Poetry Children Write* (see Bibliography).

8 Getting Words onto the Page

Your students have written texts—poetry, narratives, observations, dialogues—and have experimented with ways to create visual environments that resonate with their words. They have learned how to construct basic bindings—accordion, pamphlet, stab-bound—which can be altered in various ways to suit the themes or stage the subjects they've selected. So how do you get the actual words on the pages?

The first thing students should do is to make a mock-up or model of their book in the same size as the finished project. Then they can write out their text on Post-it® Notes—a line on each note—to move around on their mock-up pages or even on their surfaced papers. This helps them to visualize how much and where the text will be on each page. It's important for students to write out their texts as a draft, have someone else (who can spell) proofread it, and then proceed. After taking such care to create environment, select materials, and design a bound volume, a careless misspelling or ungrammatical construction sticks out like a neon light.

The strategies for designing and printing or marking pages with literary content vary, depending on the amount of text an artist's book will contain. The following suggestions for getting text onto the page include blocks of words—continuous lines, stanzas, sentences, paragraphs—and individual words or phrases that highlight, echo, or add a refrain to the main writing.

Hand Lettering

With penmanship mostly ignored in the lower grades, good handwriting has become the exception rather than the rule and students will often complain that they can't or shouldn't write on their beautifully surfaced papers. Without studying calligraphy, they can easily follow a few guidelines that will greatly improve their hand lettering. Have your students write out the alphabet between lines, all in capitals and then in lower case, and look for characteristics of style.

- *is there a slant to the letters?*
- *are the letters tall? thin? angular? rounded? short? wide?*
- *is the lettering compressed or are the letters widely spaced?*
- *are cross-bars high or low?*
- *are there distinctive eccentricities that can be emphasized? (or should be de-emphasized?)*
- *are the ascenders (stems up) and descenders (stems down) short or long?*

With these questions answered and the handwriting analyzed, the student should practice this "style," and then write his text on lines with a monoline tool (e.g. a fine line marker, a gel pen, a cartridge or fountain pen; ball-point pens are not recommended). The goal should be consistency, legibility and neatness. A few examples of monoline alphabets follow. Since artists' books are personal statements, emphasize the value of handwritten text. In fact, if you look at students' doodles, they often stylize their writing to look spooky and "gothic," nervous, angry, puffy and cloudlike, and shadowed. These techniques might come in handy for a particular theme or text. If drawing and erasing lines put on the page won't work for a particular project, try working on a light box on which you've placed a sheet that is lined. If the paper is too thick or dark to show lines through a light box, use a sheet of paper as your line. Write the text above the paper "line" and later fill in the descending strokes (i.e. the bottom of lower case p, g, y, etc.).

A few final words about hand-lettering:

- Encourage students to pencil in their words, have them proofread, and then write them out in ink.
- Sharpie® markers are popular but will bleed on certain papers. Test any marker on the same paper that is being used for the final project and on a similar surface (e.g. watercolor wash, chalk marbling, etc.). Workable matte fixative sprayed on the paper before writing will often prevent bleeding.

ABCDEFGHIJKLM
NOPQRSTUVWXYZ
abcdefghijklmn
opqrstuvwxyz

ABCDEFGHIJKLM
NOPQRSTUVWXYZ
abcdefghijklm
nopqrstuvwxyz

ABCDEFGHIJKLM
NOPQRSTUVWXYZ
abcdefghijklmn
opqrstuvwxyz

Computer Type

With the vast numbers of typefaces now readily available on personal computers, it's simple to "set type" for the artist's book. The easiest way to do this is to print directly on the pages of the book, but this limits the size, shape, surface, and type of the paper to be used in the book. Depending on the printer being used, some of the paper environments (e.g. paste paper, stencil, chalk marbling) may not be suitable and might even cause damage. A few simple ways around this are:

- setting the text in a box that will be incorporated into the design of the page and pasted on after printing
- printing the text onto colored paper that is similar to the shade of the surfaced page and then cutting out strips or blocks, gluing it onto the page and adding some color or pattern with colored pencils to camouflage the additions
- printing the text onto translucent or transparent sheets (that are compatible with the printer) and attaching them to pages as overlays

However the computer is used in producing artists' books, students should be cautioned against using the most outlandish, weird, or unreadable typeface they can find. Rather than displaying individual style, this tends to repel the viewer from interacting with the text. Another design tip is to limit the choice of typefaces to two within a project. Too many different styles within a small book reads as chaos.

Rubber Stamp Letters

Rubber stamp alphabets have gotten quite sophisticated in recent years and are readily available and affordable at arts and crafts stores. Since it's challenging to line up individual letters for a printed line, look for stamp sets that include a way to lock letters together to make a word or line of words. Or, if regular spacing and straight lines

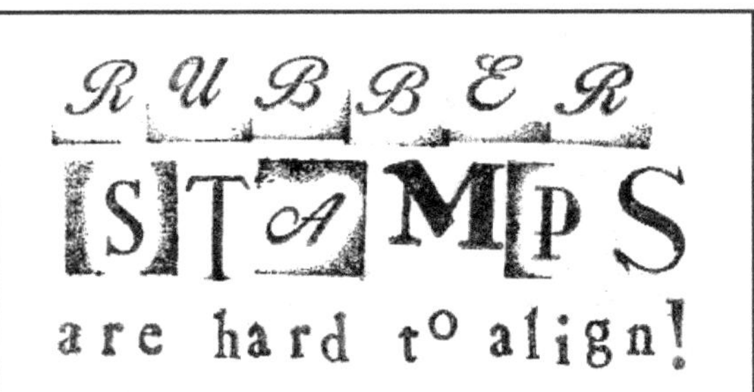

don't matter for a particular project, go for the charm and hands-on look of hand-printed words. As with computer type, students should limit the number of different styles of rubber stamp alphabets within one project, but the sizes of these stamps can be varied as well as the color stamped onto the page.

Stencils

Those old-fashioned stencils cut out of tag board that we Baby Boomers used for school posters and report covers are very useful for getting text onto pages, especially when used together with another form of lettering as a contrast. There are plastic templates with different style alphabets available at office supply stores and even at dollar stores. At arts and crafts shops, some fancier templates made out of brass are sold for embossing, but can also be used for stenciling. The size of the letters in the stencil may dictate the tool to use; e.g. a pointed colored pencil or very fine line marker would work for thin monoline stencils, while a stencil brush and paint would work for larger "headline" type stencils. If you plan to use paint or water soluble markers, however, and the stencil is made of tag board or card stock, remember to cover both sides of the stencil with clear Con-Tact® paper to make it waterproof. You'll have to cut out the letters with an X-acto® knife.

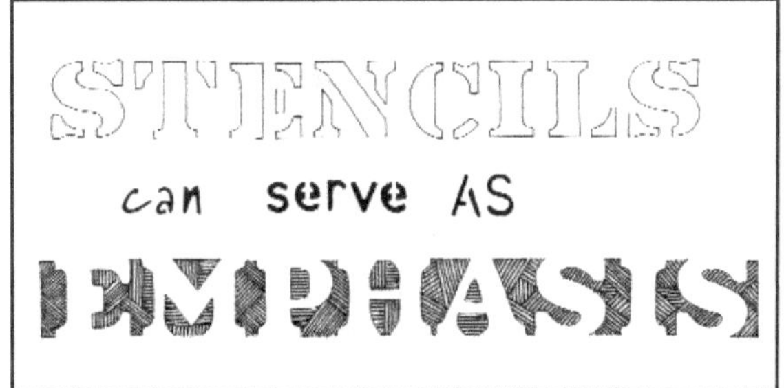

Ransom Note Collage

Forming words by gluing down letters cut from different publications, a là ransom notes, may not be the best technique for a lyrical or graceful text, but its look lends quirkiness to a compatible theme. Avoid newsprint: it smears when pasted down. If you need the letters found in a newspaper, photocopy them first and then paste the copies. Glossy magazine print is ideal.

Masking

Although this would not be a good way to letter a lengthy text (more than a few words), masking out a key word that echoes, counterpoints, or contradicts the main text is an effective way to add interest to a page. Masking can be done in several simple ways.

Crayon Resist: The white crayon resist method is done exactly the way it is described on page 27 as a way to create environment on the paper. The only disadvantage to this technique is that writing over waxy crayon is difficult at best. If you choose to use crayon resist to augment your main text, you might carefully scratch away the wax with an X-acto® knife, to allow writing on top of the crayon, or iron the back of the sheet face-down on absorbent towels

Erased Graphite: Powdered graphite is available in jars at art supply stores, or at the bottom of your pencil sharpener, if you care to sift out the wood shavings! Sprinkle some graphite on a piece of paper and lightly rub it in with gestural strokes. Then run it under a thin stream of water in the sink to further move around the graphite particles. Most of the sheet will have a gray tone, darker in places, patterned where you've rubbed it in and where the stream of water has hit it. Shake off the rest of the graphite (don't rub or brush it off). When the paper is completely dry, you can write words with an eraser, which leaves the white paper showing through. This technique can be subtle, dramatic, and mysterious. You should plan to spray the sheet with a workable fixative (outdoors or with lots of ventilation) so that the graphite doesn't continue to smear and so that you can add additional text on top of it.

Masking Fluid: There are several brands* of this rubbery liquid that you can paint on, allow to dry thoroughly, and then paint over. When the paint is dry, the mask rubs off like rubber cement. In fact, rubber cement can also be used if it's thinned down, but its toxic fumes and tendency to stain paper makes it less desirable. There are two main problems with using masking fluid: you must first coat your brush with soapy water, or you'll never get it clean again; you should experiment with it on the paper you plan to use for pages because it tears some papers when it is rubbed off. However, when it works, masking fluid is a terrific method for layering messages that seem to be receding into the paper. If fine letterforms aren't necessary for the message being masked out, you can use disposable sticks or Q-tips®. And, since the latex acts like an eraser, you can even lightly letter in pencil on the paper, cover the lines with masking fluid, and the pencil lines will be removed when you rub it off.

Stencil Mask: Another way to incorporate text onto a surfaced paper is to plan where you want the words to be placed on the page and mask off that area with a stencil cut from paper and adhered with low-tack tape. Post-it® Notes can be used for stencils as well as wide painters' tape, which is removable and won't disturb the surface of the paper. This is especially effective for watercolor environments, sumi and chalk marbling, spatter and spray paint.

Emboss

As was described with embossing shapes on page 28, words can also be embossed onto the page. Two things are essential: always work from the back of the paper and remember to reverse your word so that it reads correctly from the front. As with all embossing, a stencil needs to be cut from a sheet of heavy paper (cover weight). For letters that have a portion that drops out when you cut it (e.g. the center of an 'O' or the triangle above the cross bar of an 'A'), save the piece, back the stencil with wax paper (or another thin translucent paper), and

* Some brands of masking liquid include: Incredible White Mask (Grafix); Art Maskoid; Miskit (Grumbacher); Art Masking Fluid (Winsor and Newton); Pebeo Drawing Gum; and Masquepen Art Masking Fluid.

glue the missing piece onto the translucent backing with a glue stick. Cutting a lot of these stencils will take a long time and may be tedious, so I suggest selecting important words to highlight or echo the rest of the text.

Another way to use this technique for text purposes is to emboss a channel or a thick line across each page, varying its position to avoid monotony, and writing text within that space.

Embossing will only work with dry media or after water-based media dries. If, for example, you emboss a word and then try marbling the paper, the embossing will stretch out and disappear in the water.

9 Artist Book Projects

Preface

The directions for each of the following activities suggest starting with the content or starting with the form, or working with the two simultaneously, or trying it either way. This is intentional: every choice your students make will alter the outcome of their books. The same project can be repeated with a different starting point and result in a completely different piece of work. We'll be giving specific directions for size and materials to start you off, but these can easily be altered to individualize the artists' books. At the end of some of the projects, we will suggest ways to alter the activity in order to tailor it to a different curriculum, reuse it with the same group, or change focus from form to content or from content to form.

You should familiarize yourself with the basic instructions for accordion fold, pamphlet stitched, and stab-bound books that are given in Chapter 6. These basic instructions will not be repeated within the following projects, but will be referred to. Alterations to these instructions will, however, be thoroughly explained. The projects are ordered roughly in terms of bookbinding skill—from easiest to more challenging—but no activity is beyond the abilities of an interested novice. Now the fun begins: enjoy!

Note:

The "Basic Bookbinding Kit" referred to in the lists of materials for these projects is described on page 60.

Beach book with driftwood binding & shells.

Project #1: Environmental Album

Overview:

In this project, the form and the content are developed simultaneously. The "Environment" in the title can refer to a place or to a time. The finished book will be 6 × 9″ (horizontal format) and stab-bound in its simplest form: no sewing or gluing! Students can brainstorm visually and verbally about a theme, compile the pages, and bind the book without much concern about technical skill or grammatical correctness. This is an easy project for young or reluctant students and is all about picking a topic and developing it.

Materials:

- 1 sheet of 9 × 12″ construction or coverweight paper
- 10 sheets of 9 × 12″ drawing paper
- ¼″ hole punch
- Basic Bookbinding Kit, minus the glue
- a rubber band
- a stick or pencil that is 5-7″ long
- paper surfacing supplies

Procedure:

1. Choose an environment (e.g. "Spring," or "the beach").
2. Students will use paper surfacing techniques described in the previous chapter to evoke their chosen environment. For example, bubble marbling (page 31) in pink and blue resembles the blooms of hydrangeas; frottage (page 21) with a tan pencil over rough sand paper or a sidewalk provides texture that suggests a sandy beach.
3. Ten sheets of drawing paper should be treated in various ways that relate to the theme and then cut in half to yield 20 sheets that are 6 × 9″.
4. Brainstorm, individually or collaboratively, using the five senses to generate words that evoke the theme. Have your students close their eyes and picture themselves at a beach, in the woods, at an amusement park in the middle of summer. Go around the room and lightly tap students on the arm, asking "What do you see at your beach?" "What do you smell?" etc. Have them speak in the present tense and engage all five of their senses. Be sure to ask students to include details in their responses such as color, texture, pungency of scent. I often ask for elaboration: "Is the sand you are feeling grainy or soft?" "Is the water cold or warm?" You can follow this brainstorming by having students construct a collaborative "It's About" poem.

Forest book with evergreen twig binding.

5. When your class has completed a model poem, you might want to use this exercise to note the way repetition of words and phrases can be used to create rhythm.
6. You can follow this practice poem by asking students to create a poem about their environment using this format or a different form of their own choosing. Stress use of sensory detail employing all five senses.
7. Back to the form: with the paper held horizontally, leave one inch along the left margin without writing, since this area will be hidden by the binding.
8. Add writing to the pages (Note: not all pages need to have words, but each page needs to relate to the book), allowing the paper surfacing to help with design and placement of the text.
9. Cut the sheet of cover paper in half to make two pieces, each 6× 9″.
10. Order the pages and place a cover sheet on the top and bottom of the stack.
11. Clip the sheets together with two clothespins.
12. From the left side (or spine) of the book, measure in ½″ and lightly draw a margin line on the back cover. (Later, it can be erased.)
13. Punch 2 holes, 1½″ down from top and 1½″ up from the bottom along the margin line. This will need to be done a few sheets at a time, unless you have a fancy ¼″ drill punch.
14. From the back, insert one end of the rubber band through the bottom hole and put the stick or pencil through the loop of rubber band on the front cover. Insert the other end of the rubber band, again from the back, through the top hole, and insert the stick or pencil.
15. Optional finishing details:
    - Add a title and author line on the cover.
    - Cut a little window to show a bit of the first page through the cover.

It's about...

Directions for the "It's About" Poem

- Ask students to choose a familiar place or activity (e.g., Disneyworld, a baseball game)
- Write the words "It's about" at the left side of the blackboard and then ask students to suggest 3 things one might hear at this place. Remind students to include descriptive/detail words. Write these as a list.
- Again start your stanza with "It's about" and then ask for 3 scents which you will list.
- Repeat this format for each sense.
- You can use the 5 senses in any order. I like to point out to students that where they start might relate to what comes to mind first when the place is pictured. When I enter a zoo, for example, I often first notice the smell.
- An example:

The Beach

It's about the crash of waves on rocks
the squawk of seagulls
the shrill lifeguard whistle
It's about the scent of dead fish
the sweet coconutty suntan lotions
and hot dogs with mustard
It's about bright red umbrellas
children playing with buckets
and shells along the breaker line
It's about the hot, coarse sand
cold, slapping water
and a soft towel under your back
It's about sweet roasted marshmallows
tuna fish sandwiches from the cooler
and the salty taste of the sea.

- Change the stick or pencil into something that relates to the theme, e.g. a piece of driftwood, a sprig of pussy-willow, a popsicle stick, a chopstick, etc.
- Decorate the binding by tying some threads or yarn around whatever type of stick was used and attaching charms, beads, feathers, shells, or small artifacts that relate to the theme.

Alternative applications:

This project can be used to explore and develop ideas about geographical environments (e.g. the rainforest), literary locales (e.g. Middle Earth), historical periods (Elizabethan England), even prehistoric times. An album of this sort gives students the opportunity to combine research and imagination in developing a visual representation of a theme.

Project #2: Unfolding Memories

Overview:

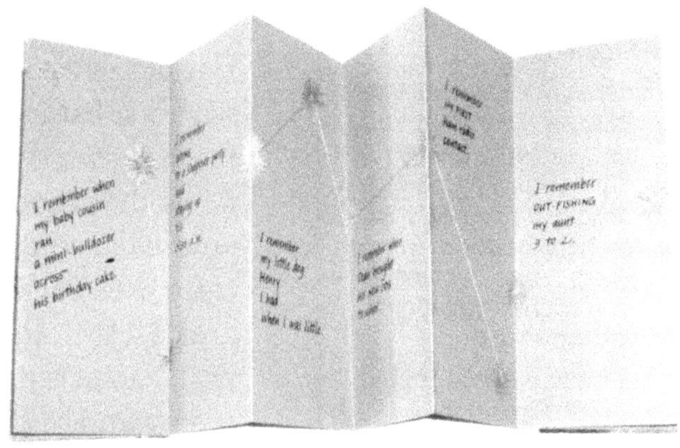

Memory Book with strings and "synapses."

The content is the initial focus of this project, and should determine the shape and size of the accordion book that will house it. We'll give specific sizes for materials, but remember that these are just suggestions to get you started. Through a guided meditation that helps recall memories, students will explore stream of consciousness in writing and discover ways to visualize it in a sequence of connected pages. The style of each writer's memory accumulation—whether short phrases or long meditative passages—will dictate the format of the book.

As writers, we often draw subject matter from our own fund of memory and personal experience. We color our writing with details of the sensory experiences of our day-to-day life. Because of this, memory writing assignments provide accessible early writing experiences for most student creative writers and make excellent beginnings for a poetry/bookmaking unit. Memories elicited are usually vivid and colorful. The material is the student's own life in all its concrete detail and down-to-earth glory. And the practice of memory writing allows students to see that poetry can be made of their own perceptions, speech patterns and usual activities.

Warming Up:

There are numerous ways to elicit the sensory details around particular memories and to encourage students to find concrete, specific language to articulate the memory. Depending on the sophistication of your students, you may want to begin by having them warm up their five senses. For example: Picture being at the beach or in the mountains and have students, with eyes closed, tell you what they are imagining themselves smelling, tasting, hearing, feeling and seeing. Encourage concrete, specific detail in the sharing of these images. What color beach ball do you see? Does the suntan lotion smell like coconuts?

Sometimes I bring scent samples as a stimulus to memory. Use opaque containers (film cannisters work well) and fill each with a substance which has a distinct, evocative scent. Vanilla, fresh mown grass, garlic, rubbing alcohol, and tobacco are just a few that tend to elicit specific memory. You can let students sniff each container and then jot down a few words they associate with each scent. Or, you can have students create a chart and list a holiday, person, season, place or event associated with each scent. You may want to just have the students sniff scents and brainstorm together, verbally sharing associations with that scent. The point is to jog memory.

For some students beginning this writing experience directly with the following guided meditation will be sufficient to elicit strong, detailed memory writing.

Guided Meditation

When students are ready to begin focusing their memories and creating scenes, it is time to walk them through a guided meditation (see sidebar). Have students sit comfortably and close their eyes as you guide them toward creating an image of a significant room of early childhood. When you have finished, give them five minutes to jot down images. Remind students to include concrete detail and to use all five senses to envision this room.

Students can be instructed to shape this memory material in a variety of ways. One easy, enjoyable created form is the "I Remember" poem. Instruct students to start each line with the words "I remember" and follow this phrase with one specific experience, moment or vision. (I remember the smell of play dough in my kindergarten classroom. I remember stretching onto tippy toes to reach the water fountain when I was five.)

A variation of the "I Remember" poem is to have students begin with the phrase "I remember" but concentrate on the details of one particular memory of a place or experience.

One memory often evokes another. A whiff of vanilla may remind us of Christmas cookies at Aunt Bev's which in turn may evoke a memory of Aunt Bev's black Lab and the time he almost knocked you over when you were two and how you

Guided Meditation

- With your eyes closed, picture a room that was significant to you when you were a very young child. This may be your first bedroom, a room in your grandmother's house or in your best friend's house, a place where you spent a vacation when you were five.
- Let your interior eye become a movie camera "panning" around this room. Look at the room from floor to ceiling, from right wall to left, from back to front.
- What objects do you see in this room? What object/furnishing is most prominent or noticeable?
- What colors do you see in this room?
- Is the room cluttered or spare and open?
- What scents do you notice when you inhale deeply?
- What sounds are you hearing in the room? From outside the room?
- Are you in the room as you picture it? Are you in the room alone? With others? Who is in this room or is it empty?
- What textures do you feel as you glide a hand over surfaces in this room?
- What is the quality of light in the room? From windows? From a hallway? From fixtures inside the room?
- When you have fixed an image of this room in your mind, open your eyes, pick up your pen and begin to jot down some of the details of what you noticed on this mental trip around the room. Try to list details which involve as many of your five senses as you can.

cried when your best friend, who also had a black Lab, moved away. I like to remind students that memories unfold, thread together, flow.

The book form that also unfolds from page to page and when opened completely reveals an entire flow of thought is the Accordion Book.

Materials:

- 2 pieces of chipboard or mat board (for covers), each 3¼ × 9¼″
- paper for pages, colored or white, 18 × 24″ (an 18 × 24″ sheet will yield two sets of pages, each 9 × 24″)
- 2 sheets of paper to cover boards, each 4¾ × 10¾″
- Basic Bookbinding Kit
- colored thread, ~2 yards, to contrast with the color of the pages
- writing tools for recording memories onto pages
- optional: colored pencils, gel pens

Procedure:

1. After text has been written and revised, students will make an accordion book as directed in Chapter 6. Cover the boards with cover paper and press under heavy books until dry. Fold the 9 × 24″ sheet into 8 panels (each 3″ wide).
2. Arrange the memory writing on the 8 pages. Tip: Post-it® notes are a great way to move text around on a set of pages. For this book, vary the placement of text from page to page.
3. Write on the pages, allowing space between entries.
4. In this space between entries, you will sew a line of stitching that connects one entry to the next, periodically indicating a "synapse" of sorts, by accenting the point where the thread disappears into the page with colored pencil or gel pen "fireworks."
5. When the pages are complete, and the covers are dry and pressed, glue the outside of the first and last panels of the accordion pages into the covers and press again.

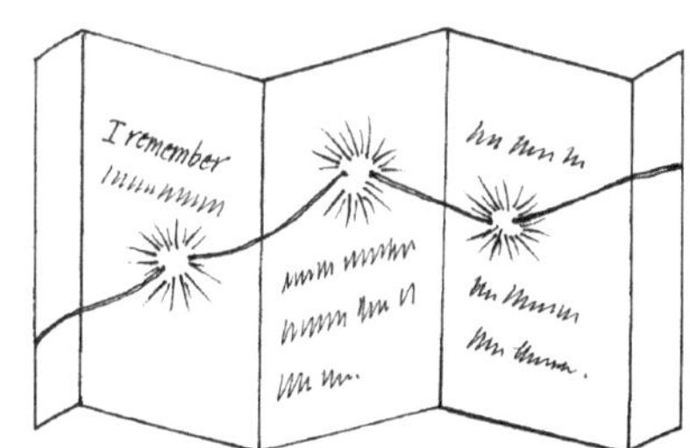

Accordion memory book with threads and "fireworks"

Alternative applications:

Instead of using their own memories, students could write in the character of an historical person—real or imagined—who is recalling events that happened in his lifetime (e.g. a Union or Rebel soldier approaching the Battle of Gettysburg, fighting, surviving, and being sent home wounded).

PROJECT #3: "IT WAS A DARK AND STORMY NIGHT..."

Overview:

Hardcover pamphlet.

In this project, content is developed and then a book is constructed to house the poem. As the title of the project suggests, content is jump-started by an opening created by another author. The pamphlet book form seems a natural match for the narrative poem as both are laid out in familiar and fairly linear ways, though both can be altered to underscore the tone or meaning of the tale being told.

This is not strictly an artist's book, but the more students try to relate the covering materials, colors, tools for writing, and any embellishments to the theme, the more it will be a true marriage of content and form.

One way to answer the "I don't know where to start" complaint is to give students the opening of their piece of writing, to suggest beginning by responding to what someone has else already put on the page. You can find great opening lines everywhere. Jot down favorite lines from magazine articles, stories, poems. Put quotes onto file cards and hold onto them.

Introducing Narrative Writing:

All students tell stories. At the end of a day, a boy or girl might sit on the school bus and tell a friend about an incident on the playground. Over lunch on a typical Monday, students will recount adventures they had over the weekend. These stories are constructed of natural speech and are often lively and vivid since the storyteller is invested in conveying both the facts of and the feelings surrounding the experience.

When I work with students on writing narratives, I remind them that they are used to recounting stories, and that the best place to start to write a narrative poem is by capturing speech onto paper. *Write it down the way you would say it and go from there* is a direction I frequently offer.

When asked what they think are the differences between poetry and fiction, many students believe that poems describe a scene or a feeling, whereas the purpose of fiction is to tell a story. Narrative poetry is poetry that tells a tale in much the same way a novel does. What differs is the manner of telling. The narrator uses the tools of the poet: figurative language to describe the scene; cuts in connective tissue (transitional material) which have the effect of condensing the narrative down to the most intense details; thoughts broken into lines and stanzas rather than paragraphs; and rhythmic word and syllable choices so that writing is imbued with musicality.

Warming Up:

Journaling is a form of warming up one's narrative-making brain. Have students write about a particular part of the previous day, the most recent holiday as it was celebrated in their home, something a pet did which they found funny; any tale will do. Give a time limit but tell the students to put the pen to the page and keep it moving the whole time.

You can warm up for this writing more directly by giving an opening line to the whole class and having the group respond to it aloud. Opening lines of poems set up expectations about what will come next. Go through any of your own poetry anthologies and look for work that is not immediately familiar. (Most readers will know what follows "Two roads diverged in a yellow wood" and their minds will leap to the next line as soon as the first line is read.)

Read a few lines aloud and give students a chance to brainstorm about what they expect the rest of the poem will be about. You might want to have students write down a few ideas of what they believe the poem is about before the discussion begins or you may simply want to list ideas on the board as students call them out. One of my personal favorites is an untitled poem[1] which opens

Like magic
thin green sticks

Like magic
thin green sticks

I write those two lines on the blackboard and have students brainstorm about those sticks. We list all the things the sticks

[1] Joanne Ryder, *The Place My Words Are Looking For*, p. 104

might be: celery, grass, stems, pick-up sticks, magic wands, green beans, mantis bodies, licorice, crayons. Encourage students to stretch their imaginations.

Here's a wonderful example of how one of our students responded to this prompt:

Like magic thin green sticks,
the grass danced on the breeze that night.
The wind swept the freshly cut grass into its arms
and waltzed away with it.
I stood barefoot on the wooden steps of my back porch,
letting the magic brush my face and hair.
The only noise was the howling of the North Wind
singing to the dance of the grass.
The smell swept my senses,
clearing my head to an empty dizziness.
My chest tightened as my breath knocked from me,
and I just stood there,
letting my spirit dance with it all.

—Maura Roche, age 15

Writing the Narrative Poem:

After the brainstorming session, you might want to have students use the lines you have already discussed to write their own poems. Alternatively, you might want to read them the rest of the warm up poem and then give students a choice of several other first lines from which to construct their own poems. With younger students or less fluent writers, consider having students write from the lines already discussed; in this case the discussion will literally have them cooking up ideas.

This is one assignment for which collaboration should be discouraged. Tell your students that the "game" is to see how many different ideas they can generate from a common first line.

If students want guidelines or structure, point out how the first line is written and suggest that the rest of the poem might be written to "fit with" the structure set up in the opening. This is an opportunity for you as a teacher to sensitize students to the ways authors set tone, suggest voice, and begin to unfold meaning with the all-important first words of a piece of writing.

For more sophisticated writers, try offering students a last line to write toward. Make sure to have all the students read the stories they create to each other. Everyone will be amazed at all the paths that have been taken to arrive at the same destination.

Procedure:

The procedure for making this book is described in Chapter 6, even using the same size materials. Follow the directions for the hardcover pamphlet. As in any artist book, the selection of cover paper, the size and shape of the book, the choice of paper for pages, the writing materials used, the color and design of the pages should relate to the overall theme in some way, or at least not distract from it. Even the arrangement of the text on the page is a choice that can affect the visual reception by the reader (e.g. short choppy lines vs. dense, lengthy text vs. one line strung across a page).

Materials:

- Basic Bookbinding Kit
- 5 sheets of 8½ × 11″ paper
- 2 sheets of 8½ × 11″ colored paper (endpapers)
- cardstock hinge, 3 × 8½″
- bookcloth, 3 × 10″
- 2 pieces chipboard or mat-board, 5 ¼ × 8 ½″
- 2 pieces cover paper, 5 × 10″

Alternative Applications:

There are several ways to vary this project, some involving writing and others involving the book format. First, the alternative writing prompts:

- Instead of having students write narrative in response to a first line, you could have them write a narrative from the point of view of an historic figure or of an historic period. Remind them to use language appropriate to that time.
- Use a line from a science text as the opening of a poem. For example, the description of photosynthesis can sound magical. If you are studying weather, have students write poems using atmospheric words to figuratively set the atmosphere of their story.
- Use opening and closing lines of literature not yet read by the students but which you will read in English classes. Have students construct their own tales and discuss what sorts of expectations are set up by the language of these lines. Later

you can discuss in what ways these expectations were or were not realized.

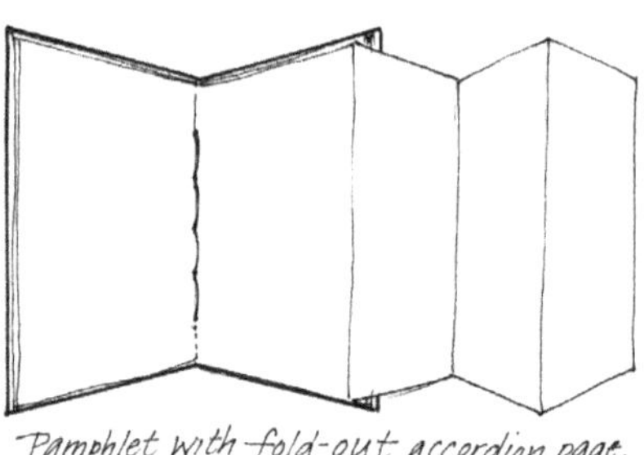
Pamphlet with fold-out accordion page.

- Hand out your file card quotations (see page 100) and ask students to use the quote they were given as an epigraph. Explain that an epigraph is a quotation that comes at the beginning of a poem, story, or memoir and suggests a theme of the writing which follows.
- Another variation uses headlines from a newspaper or magazine as the jump-start. Cut out a number of headlines and put these in a bowl or bag. Have students select a headline and use it as either their first lines of the poem or as the title of the piece. This can become quite a riot when headlines from tabloids are used. In fact, if you have a particularly quiet class, you can often generate both ideas and laughter if you use tabloid headlines in your warm up/brainstorming session.
- Even though this is a most conservative-looking book, it can also be altered to suit a particular text. The easiest alteration is to use a much wider piece of paper for one or more of the pages. These can also be folded and sewn in with the rest of the signature, but they can be accordion folded to open out when the center fold is reached, or at another point in the book. Likewise, a flap at the top or bottom of the page can be attached, concealing and then revealing an image or word. Windows and doors can be cut into pages. A pocket containing an artifact or piece of text can be attached to a page; it will interrupt the narrative flow, but this might be just what the artist wants. And finally, pages can be colored, textured, embossed, etc. before they are bound.

- Since the pages are a standard size, consider having the students edition their work, i.e. run off copies of the pages and bind each set individually so that there will be a "print run" of several copies to exchange with classmates, give to the library, or use as a gift.

Dos-à-dos

Materials:

- 5 sheets of 8½ × 11″ paper
- 1 sheet of cover-weight stock, 5 ½ × 14″
- Basic Bookbinding Kit, minus the glue

Project #4: He Said/She Said

Overview:

The *dos-à-dos* form (it means "back to back" in French) is just two pamphlet-stitched signatures inserted into the same cover, but in opposite directions. The utility of this form is that it visually represents opposition, dialogue, or any theme that can be stated as a duality. The next project (French door) will also lend itself to contrasting two themes, but because of the arrangement of the pages in the *dos-à-dos*, two opposing points of view are most effectively presented in this type of binding.

Because this project and the next one both deal with dualities or dichotomies—sometimes in opposition and sometimes in complementary terms—the writing prompts suitable to use with both book forms will be similar. Therefore, writing warm up suggestions and prompts suitable to either Project 4 or Project 5 will be offered in a separate short section immediately after this chapter and before the next (page 109).

Procedure:

Note: You may want to have students write out their text on the pages before assembling the book; it insures against messing up a page that's already been sewn into the cover.

1. Cut the 5 sheets of 8 ½ × 11″ paper in half so that you have 10 pieces of paper that are 5½ × 8½″.
2. Fold 2 signatures: 5 sheets of paper in each. The folded signatures will measure 5½″ high by 4¼″ wide.
3. From one end of the strip of cover-weight paper, measure in 4½″ and score a line with the bone folder. Fold along that score line. [*NOTE*: If possible, make sure that you are folding with the grain of the paper. This needs to be checked before you cut the strip of cover weight stock.]
4. Measuring in from the fold, score another line 4½″ in and fold again, this time in the opposite direction, so that, from the top, the folded cover looks like a "Z".
5. The cover folds have created 3 segments; the 3rd will be a little bit longer than the first two. Cut off the excess from the 3rd segment so that all three parts are equal.

6. At this point, students should write out their oppositional texts on the two signatures, including any illustrations, photos, and designs. They may want to use the first page of each signature as a title page for the section, or an introduction such as "He Said..." and "She Said...". In a book of this kind, either side can be opened first, depending on how it's held, so the artist should enable the reader to begin from either side. Discussion of writing prompts follows this section.

My Own Little World

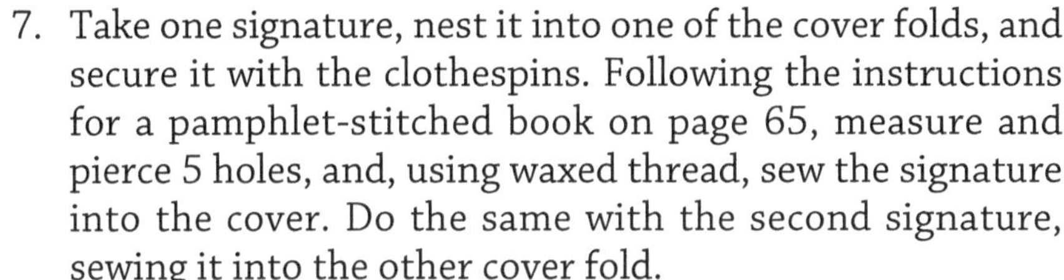

7. Take one signature, nest it into one of the cover folds, and secure it with the clothespins. Following the instructions for a pamphlet-stitched book on page 65, measure and pierce 5 holes, and, using waxed thread, sew the signature into the cover. Do the same with the second signature, sewing it into the other cover fold.
8. Remember: if you start sewing from the outside, you will end up making your knot on the outside and will have the opportunity to make a tassel, or add beads or other embellishments to the exposed binding. Other finishing details might include:
   - adding a title bar to one or both of the covers
   - covering the stitching on the spines (if sewn from the inside) with strips of decorative paper, cloth, trim, etc. [*NOTE*: Any decorative trim or embellishment, however, should relate in some way to the content of the book.]

Alternative applications:

So much educational material can be presented in the form of debate (e.g. democracy vs. totalitarianism, abstract vs. representational art). The *dos-à-dos* book is a wonderful way to organize this information and have students engage with it creatively.

You may find this project particularly useful when you are discussing diverse cultures. If you have students who are bilingual or bi-cultural, or a multi-cultural class, you might assign students to write about the contrasts and similarities in their cultures.

Adolescents often are grappling with issues of identity too. What parts of their family culture do they hope to retain or repeat? In what ways are they different from their family members? This assignment can be assigned as part of lessons aimed at self awareness and responsible choice-making as well.

Writing Prompts for Projects 4 and 5

Warming Up:

Once the *dos-à-dos* or French door book has been constructed, ask your students to examine the form and brainstorm about what the form suggests to them. Lead the discussion toward the concept of dualities. List all the dichotomies/dualities on a blackboard as students call these out. Some examples: summer and winter, night and day, my version (he said) vs. her version (she said).

You might want to have each student choose a duality of his own to develop immediately after this session, or you may want to use another warm up. I borrow an idea from Kenneth Koch[2] of having students construct and share simple contrast poems before launching into a more personal, individual choice. Have students consider "how they used to be when they were younger vs. how they are now." For more sophisticated students you might want to ask how they seem to be to the world as opposed to how they see themselves inside. Then plug ideas into the following repeated two line format:

I used to be (what?)
But now I am (what by comparison?)

The all important direction here is to use metaphor, not generic description. If you used to be small and now are bigger, you can *show* this by telling your reader you used to be a guppy, but now you are a whale. If you used to have little knowledge but now have much more, you could write, "I used to be a page, but now I am a book." These are the sorts of examples I give students before I set them to writing. This is a warm up poem and you might want to limit the writing time to 5 minutes and then have students share a few examples out loud.

I like to use a third warm up activity. I have a bowl of questions typed out on strips of paper which ask students to liken themselves to contrasting objects, seasons, activities etc. Some examples: Are you more like an ocean or a stream? Are you more like a farm or a city? I go around the room and ask stu-

[2] Kenneth Koch, *Wishes, Lies, & Dreams*

dents to randomly choose a question and answer it. There are no right answers but whatever the student chooses should be supported by some reason.

Writing Text for the Two-Section Book Forms

Ask students to write text in two parts which relate to or answer each other. A *dos-à-dos* book is back to back and this suggests that the two voices in the book are in opposition to each other. The French door book, with its side by side parts suggests that the two voices are in dialogue with each other. For both books, students will be asked to create two-part text in which the two parts are linked. Some suggested voices students could choose:

- Carry on directly from the question slips and have students write about how they are like one choice and unlike the other (*dos-à-dos*) or like one choice in some ways and like the other in other ways (French door form.)
- Create two other voices: parent/child dialogue (or contrast in point of view), imaginary vs. real activity, two friends sharing what they could do with a day, or even an internal argument over a choice an individual has to make (Do I stay in bed all day? Go to the beach? etc.). This assignment has been referred to by the poet Leslie Ullman[3] as "The Self has it Out with the Self."

[3] *The Practice of Poetry*, Leslie Ullman

Project #5: French Door Dialogue

French door Book

Overview:

The same way a French door uses two smaller doors to access one common opening, this version of a pamphlet-stitched binding visually represents two ways to enter into a common theme. Again, this simple binding is two pamphlet-stitched signatures sewn into the folds of one cover. Unlike the *dos-à-dos*, both sides of this book open from the front. Depending on how this book is held, howver, the pages can be assembled side by side or one section on top and one section below. We mention this because we've had students who chose to contrast what's going on above ground/underground, or upstairs/downstairs, and the top-bottom arrangement of pages facilitated these themes. Another alternative arrangement is to make one signature smaller (i.e. narrower) than the other, giving the larger one more importance. A middle-school student in one of our classes chose to contrast her real life and her imaginary life and felt that the latter was much more prominent, rich, and exciting. Her French door book had one skinny signature that listed daily activities and one larger signature that expanded this schedule into imaginative adventures.

The materials and instructions below are for a book with two equal-sized signatures, but you might mention the examples above to your students to see who will take an idea and run with it. This book form is extremely easy and, unless embellished in some way, not all that impressive looking. A more involved hardcover binding is described below along with several alterations that could "dress up" this book form.

[Note: The writing warm-ups and prompts are given on page 109, immediately preceding this project.]

Materials for softcover French door book:

- 10 sheets of paper for pages, 8½•× 11″
- 1 piece of cover stock, 11 × 17″
- Basic Bookbinding Kit, minus the glue
- optional: colored threads

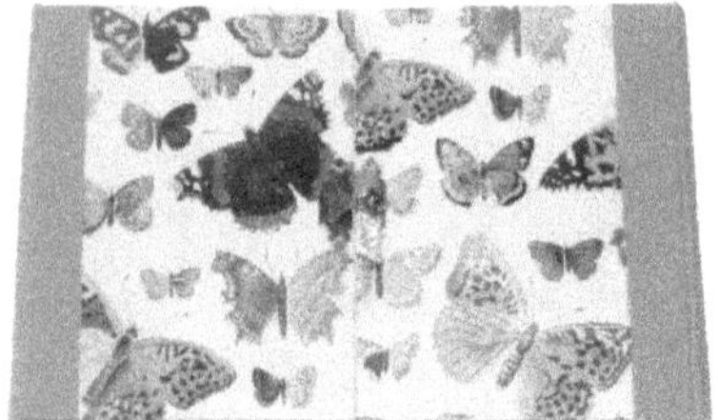

Hardcover French door book with hardware clasp.

French door book open

Procedure for softcover French door book:

1. Measure to the middle of the cover along the 17″ dimension (8½″) and mark with a dot at the top and bottom of the sheet.
2. Bring each end into the center, lining up with the dots, and fold, making the French doors.
3. Once the cover is folded, trim down the length from 11″ to 8½″, which makes the book a perfect square when closed. This easily allows the book to be presented in either a horizontal or vertical format.
4. Cut the paper for the pages down to 8 × 8 ½″. Fold two signatures, each containing 5 sheets of paper, the length of the fold = 8½″. At this point, students should write and design their pages, before sewing them into the cover. See the writing prompts for this project on page 109.
5. Take one signature, open to the center fold, nest it into one of the cover folds, and secure the pages to the cover with clothespins.
6. Measure and mark the holes for sewing in the center crease. Placing your ruler along the length of the crease, make a mark at the following points along the ruler: 1¼ ″, 2¾″, 4¼″, 5¾″, 7¼″. These marks will give you five evenly distributed stitches.
7. Pierce the marks with an awl and sew the signature into the cover using the pamphlet stitch described on page 65.
8. Repeat steps 5 – 7 with the second signature.
9. Finishing details could include adding a closure to the doors. The simplest closure is to punch a hole in the center edge of each door (toward the opening, not the fold), string a ribbon through the holes, and tie the ribbon. Another way to make an easy closure is to loop a rubber band or elastic string through a hole in one door and insert a paper fastener into the other door, around which the elastic can be stretched. If students are interested in adding a closure, just try to get them to make it in keeping with the theme of their individual books.

Alternatives:

In terms of book form, this is almost embarrassingly simple. For upper level students, art students, or a longer term project, the French door format can be done as a hardcover book, along the lines of the hardcover pamphlet in chapter 6. For a book the same size as the one described above, the measurements for a hardcover version would be as follows:

Procedure for hardcover French door book:

Follow the same procedure for making a hardcover pamphlet, with the only difference being the third cover piece which connects the two front doors to the back. After pages are sewn to the cardstock hinges, boards are glued to the hinges, bookcloth is pasted over the spines, the covering paper is applied to the two front covers in the same way (mitered corners), but the piece covering the back is just pasted onto the board with the top ¾″ folded over the top of the board and the bottom ¾″ folded over the bottom of the board. Simple!

An alternative application of this book form, whether soft or hardcover, could use the notion of doors as portals into another time or place. Students might want to depict the front covers literally as doors which allow the reader to enter into another physical space that is portrayed on the pages within.

It's possible to bind in one long sheet that can be accordion-folded.

One other project that uses this book form, combines French door with *dos-à-dos*. Using the softcover version of this book, fold the cover in half and add a third signature between the first two. Using the measurements given in this project, you'd end up with a tall skinny book, 4¼ × 8½″, that houses three individually sewn signatures.

Materials for hardcover French door book:

- 2 cardstock hinges, each 3 × 8½″
- 3 pieces of chipboard or matboard; 2 pieces that are 4 × 8½″, one piece that is 8 × 8½″
- 2 pieces of bookcloth, each 3 × 10″
- 3 pieces of covering paper; 2 pieces that are each 3¾ × 10″ and one piece that is 6 × 10″
- same paper for pages
- add 2 endpapers for each side (4 in all), same size as pages

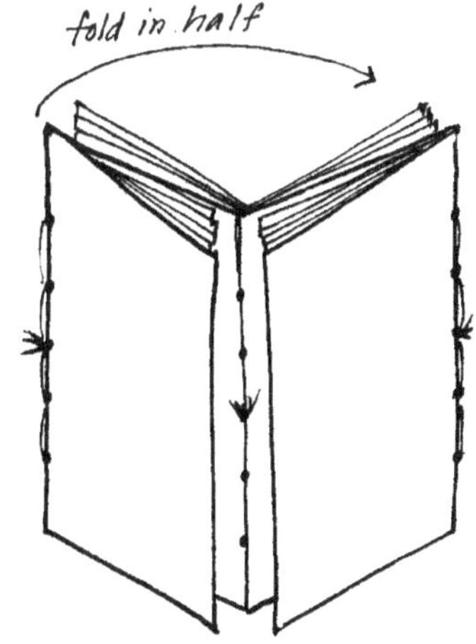

Combination form of French door and *dos-à-dos*

Project #6: "P.O.V."

Overview:

It's a challenge to convince anyone, especially an adolescent, to assume another point of view. This project takes that challenge and gets students to run with it. The book form introduced here is a pocket accordion binding, and can be used for any number of purposes. In this case, it helps to visualize how unrelated objects can have a common focus and how sequencing the text can affect the overall theme. Students will write a series of six monologues in the voices of non-human participants (e.g. pets, furniture, houseplants, etc.) that all are addressing the same situation. The situation—whether it's an argument, a party, an important announcement, an unexpected event—will be staged in the book form, with each pocket representing another "take" on the situation. Obviously, this exercise also could use the opinions/reflections of human participants, but we've found that adolescents often find it easier to express themselves imaginatively in the voice of, say, a lamp rather than a sibling (with whom there may be baggage...). Have fun with this one!

Materials:

- 2 pieces of 12 × 18″ drawing paper or acid-free construction paper
- 6 pieces of paper (any kind or color), 5 × 7″
- 2 boards, each 5¾ × 8¼″
- 2 sheets of covering paper, each 7¼″ × 9¾″
- glue stick
- Basic Bookbinding Kit

Procedure:

1. The two pieces of drawing or construction paper will have to be pieced so that you have a paper that is 12 × 33″. Here's how: along the 12″ side of one sheet, score a line 1″ in from the edge and fold along that line. With a glue stick, adhere the other sheet into the valley fold that you've just made. Now you have an expanse of paper that is 12 × 35″. Fold it where the score was made, measure 16½″ from the fold, and mark that measurement. Cut the folded paper to 16½″ long (when folded) × 12″ high. When you open up the sheet, it is now 12 × 33″. *Note: it's* ***extremely*** *important to be folding with the grain in this case. If you have paper where the grain runs along the 18″ side, find other paper with "short" grain, i.e. it runs along the 12″ length.*
2. Measure in 2½ ″ from one long side, mark, score, and fold this section up. This is your pocket.

3. From the opposite long side, measure in 1½″, mark, score, and fold down to the back of the sheet. This fold is made to equalize the thickness of the paper at the top and the bottom. If you don't make this fold, the book will not be flat when it's closed.
4. Cover the boards with the covering paper as described in Chapter 6. Press the covers under some weight.
5. With the pocket and top flap folds in place, again fold the length of the sheet in half (along the score you originally made).
6. From the fold, measure out 5½″, mark, score, and fold along that measurement. Do this on both sides of the center fold.
7. Take each of the two "raw" ends of the paper and fold these to meet the folds you just made in #6.
8. Now you have 6 pocketed panels, each of which is 5½″ wide by 8″ high.
9. The first and last pocket will need to be stitched or glued at the very end, before adhering the covers.
10. Finishing detail: Since the book itself represents a "situation" that is being commented upon, you might want to add a title to the cover to provide a context for the audience. It could be written directly on the cover, written on a title bar and adhered to the cover, or written on a "belt" that acts as a closure for the book.

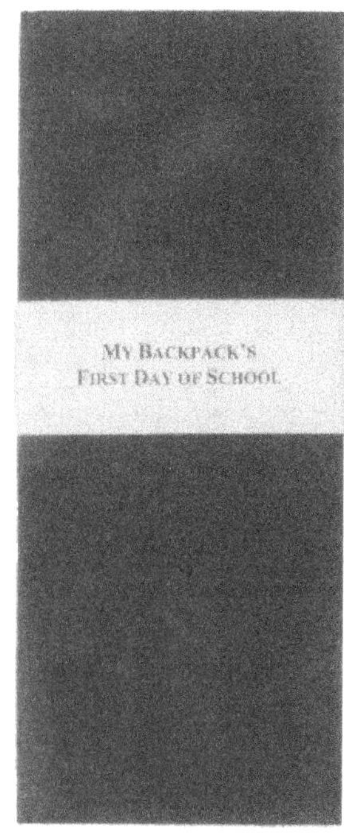

Closed Pocket Accordion with titled belt.

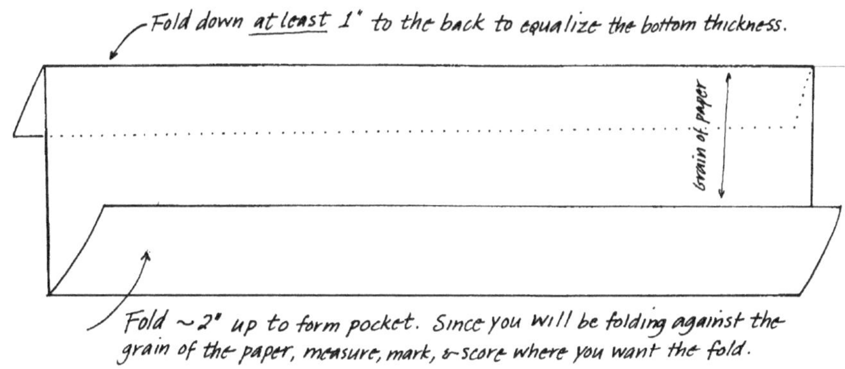

Illustration for folding paper.

Warming Up:

There are all sorts of warm up activities that will take your students out of their own points of view and into considering the point of view of someone or something else. Depending on the sophistication of your class, you may want to engage students in one or more of these.

PERSPECTIVE

- Play the tray observation game (See “My Mother’s Tray Game, p. 60) and then point out to students that the objects and the details each of them noticed literally depended on where he or she was standing and observing the tray. Write the word “PERSPECTIVE” on the board and discuss how physical perspective is changed by the student’s location in space. You can also use this activity to discuss how mindset effects what someone notices. For example, I put a Phillies Phanatic on my tray, a toy version of the Phillies baseball team mascot; students who are sports enthusiasts often comment that the Phanatic was the first item they noted.
- Have students list what they can see looking forward and what they notice if they look up or down. Have them walk around on their knees and discuss what they do not notice from down at a lower level. Have them stand on chairs and list what they notice when they get up higher.
- If you are in a school building that houses younger grade levels, you may want to ask students to return to the elementary corridor and reflect on how the rooms and hallways look different from what they remember from second grade. Again, you might want to couple this with a discussion of the definition of the word perspective.
- Have students go to a familiar place and make a list of “twenty things I never noticed.” (This can be turned directly into a list poem!)
- Rewrite a familiar scene in a piece of fiction from the point of view of a different character. One of my favorites is to have students familiar with *To Kill a Mockingbird* rewrite the trial scene from the point of view of the accuser, the accused,

the judge or even the bench itself rather than from Scout's perspective.

- Read models of monologue or voice poems. Excellent models abound and include Larry Woiwode's "Deserted Barn"[4] and Sylvia Plath's "Mushrooms"[5]. Discuss how voice and tone are created by word choices, rhythms and patterns of speech, use of colloquial or common language.

Creating Text:

Students have created a book with six pockets, six environments in which to house objects, each with its own point of view. Each student starts creating text by identifying a place in his or her house from which he or she will choose six objects.

Six individual monologues will be written. Start with draft copy and have students work on voice and tone of each so that the individual perspectives are both clear and unique. When monologues are put onto final form—the pages to be placed in the pockets—formats should also reinforce the voice and tone of the text. A scared voice might be written in a wavering hand and on wrinkled paper. A bold or rigid tone might be supported by placing text on cardboard. A student might want to fold the words of a shy speaker and "hide" them in the pocket completely so the reader has to literally pry the comments loose from the book.

Concrete Poem (*These Hands*)

These Hands

These hands can clap rhythms
These hands can speak signs
These hands can color sunset
These hands can craft sandcastles
These hands can hold other hands
These hands can...

Some students may want to create concrete poems as part of their POV books. Concrete poems are written in a shape that is relevant to the subject of the poem, e.g., a star-shaped

[4] "Deserted Barn" by Larry Woiwode, taken from Dunning & Glass, p. 97
[5] "Mushrooms" by Sylvia Plath, taken from Gensler & Nyhart, p. 82

poem about sleeping outdoors, a poem in the shape of a hand about work one does by hand. Consider encouraging students to use this as only one way to express the link between form and content. It is probably the most literal, concrete link and certainly one legitimate way to show content with form, but experimentation with other more subtle links should be encouraged.

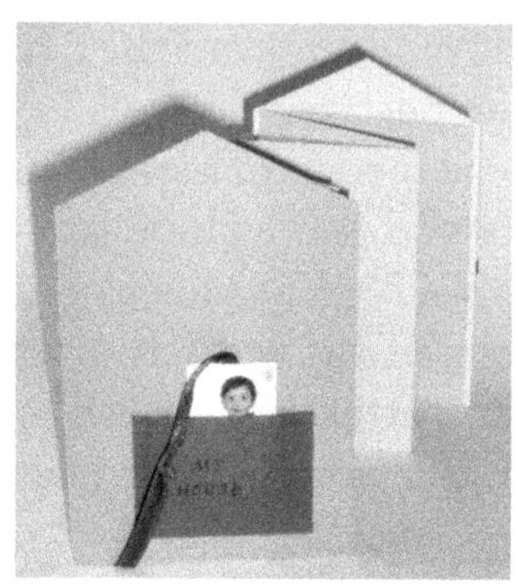

Photograph of house book

You may want to place specific limits on the length of each monologue, just to help students finish all six. Whether or not you impose limits, remind students to be aware of the space limitations of the book form and the individual pockets. Along these lines, encourage students to experiment with the order of their monologues so that they will see that sequencing can affect the tone, mood, and overall message of the text.

Alternative Applications:

With younger students, a pocket accordion book can be shaped into a house shape (cut an inverted "V" at the top of each cover, and have the "roof" extend beyond the top of the pages) so that each page can be a different room of the house. Students can then describe their place in each room. Another idea for the younger student is to call the book "My Neighborhood," and to use each pocket as a place to talk about a key location in the neighborhood—the school, library, post office, drug store, etc.

"House Book" Pocket Accordion

fold down (in the back) at least 1" to equalize the bulk at the bottom.
Photo of House
KITCHEN SINK
DINING ROOM Chandelier
LIVING ROOM SOFA
My Alarm Clock
PARENTS' ROOM DOOR
ATTIC CEDAR CHEST
Family Photo
fold up ~2" to make a pocket.
glue down edge of pocket.
Attach Ribbon to inside front & back covers so book can be tied shut.
glue edge of pocket

Project #7: Thematic Flag Book

Overview:

Many academic subjects are taught in units around particular themes. This project affords teachers an opportunity to incorporate language and book arts directly into a particular thematic unit. Students will explore the subject at hand while deepening their abilities at self expression.

Although we are presenting this as a "Content first" (rather than "Form first") project, it is important for students to understand the way the book is assembled before they finalize their writing. The Flag Book is a quirky variation of an accordion fold book that was first developed by renowned contemporary book artist Hedi Kyle. The covers are covered boards and the spine is a narrow accordion fold. The pages are small "flags" that are adhered to the folded spine in two directions so that upon opening the book, the pages pop out. Visually, it's an impressive format: students love it! However, we suggest that you make one model of the book to pass around the room so that your writers can visualize the stage for their words.

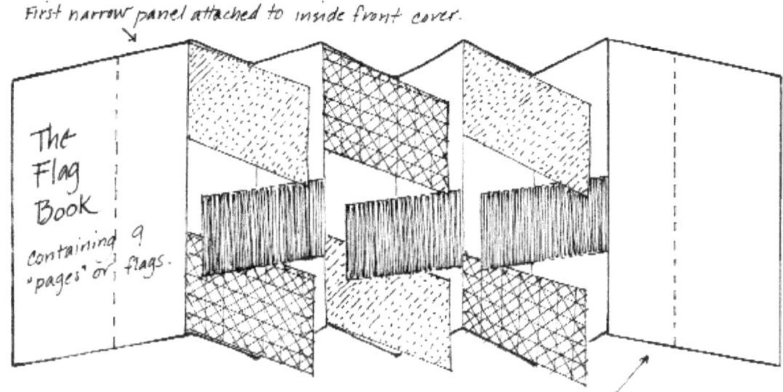

Many students struggle with making generic language vivid. The thematic flag book project underscores the need to find just the right word, the sharpest, most resonant word for a feeling or physical description or action. At the same time, it introduces a new book form.

Vivid Words

Often students' first drafts of poems, essays, or stories will contain much generic language. In revision sessions, you probably already encourage your students to seek ways to replace such non-specific, clunky language with vivid, more concrete words. *I can't see a beautiful sky*, I might tell a student, *but I can see a sky that's streaked with mauve and magenta and looks like wisps of cotton candy*. Similarly, a boy who "walks by" might be feeling all sorts of emotions; a boy who "trots over the sidewalk" is probably gleeful. An essay about an historic period, a lab report, a book report, a description or an argument essay, all of these are strengthened by concrete, specific word choices. Even a job or college application letter becomes more compelling when concrete language is used.

Warming Up

Any exercise that encourages students to use specific, concrete language works well as a warm up for this project. You might want simply to list some generic adjectives and verbs on the board and have students list synonyms which they believe are more interesting ways of saying the same thing.

This could also be a time to haul out "My Mother's Tray Game" (page 52). Ask students to list the objects they remember on the tray *in as much concrete detail as they can, using specific color, texture, size, and shape words.*

Movement warm-ups can work well with this project. If you have students who won't be too self-conscious, have them stand up and act out how "leaped for joy" moves, or "slumped and dejected" sits.

Creating Text

The first task is to define your theme. You may want to assign the whole class one theme (e.g. the Underground Railroad) or you may want to ask students to find their theme from within a broad category (any aspect of the Civil War).

Start by having students make lists of words or phrases that relate to the theme. Once the students have generated a list of perhaps thirty words and phrases, have them pick 24 which they feel are the most vivid, unusual, personally expressive. These will be written onto the flags (pages) of the flag book. You can allow students to combine words with visual images that also articulate some aspect of the theme.

You also might want to use this project as a parts of speech exercise. In this case, you can instruct your students to make three lists of words related to their topic. Students generate a list of nouns, a list of action verbs, and a list of adjectives relating to the theme and pick the most vivid of each to include in the flag book. The writing for this project can be generated individually or collaboratively, especially for younger or less articulate students.

Procedure:

1. Glue the covering paper onto the boards, miter the corners, and press (as described on page 62).
2. Cut the 11 × 17″ sheet down to 9 × 16″; it is important that the grain of the paper runs parallel to the 9″ side (see illustration in sidebar).
3. To make an accordion spine, start by folding the sheet in half horizontally so that you have two panels, each 9 × 8½″. Continue folding each panel in half until you have 16 panels, each 1″ wide × 9″ high. You don't need to measure for this; just fold neatly and accurately and the 16 panels will be the right size.
4. Write the selected words or phrases onto each of the flags on one side only. If images are to be included (e.g. small photos, maps, or drawings), glue them onto the flags as well.
5. Arrange the flags in the proper order, in groups of three.
6. On the back of each flag, draw a 1″ margin on the right side for two of the flags (the ones appearing at the top and bottom of each panel), and on the left side for the one in the middle.
7. With a glue stick, run a line of glue within that margin and adhere the first flag to the second panel, lining it up with the top of the accordion spine and flush into the fold.
8. Take the third flag, apply glue as above, and adhere it to the second panel, lining it up with the bottom of the accordion spine and flush into the fold.
9. Take the second flag, apply glue, and adhere it to the *third* panel, flush into the fold and centered between the first and third flags. Now the pages open out in two directions as desired.
10. Follow this pattern for each set of three pages (glue in the first and third, add the second on the next panel).
11. The first and last panels are blank, because they are used to attach the spine to the covers. To do this, after all the

Materials:

- 1 sheet 11 × 17″ paper, at least
  70 lb. weight
- 2 pieces of chipboard or matboard, 4¼ × 9″
- 18 pieces of fairly heavy-weight paper, at least 70 lb., 3 × 4″
- 2 pieces of covering paper, 5¾ × 10½″
- 2 sheets of lining paper (can be same as covering paper), 4 •× 8″
- Basic Bookbinding Kit
- glue stick

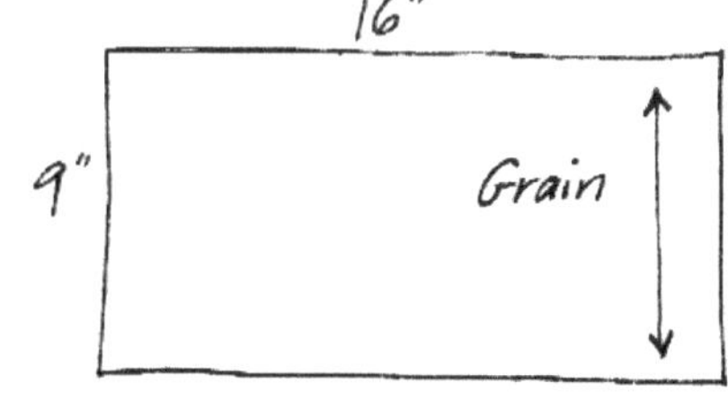

Grain of the paper runs parallel to the 9″ side

pages have been adhered into the spine, apply glue to the outside of the first panel and adhere to the inside of the front cover, flush right, lined up top and bottom. Repeat the same process with the last panel flush left on the inside cover.

12. Line the inside front and back covers by gluing the selected liner paper over the accordion panel on the inside of each cover.
13. Add a title bar to the front cover and the flag book is ready for display!

Alternative Applications

This physical format could have as few as 2 flags extending from each position on the accordion spine or many narrower flags, depending on the height of the book. Some students may prefer writing in paragraph form and the larger flags would accommodate that preference.

AA through Z, a collaborative flag book by the members of Bound Together, a women's book arts collaborative, 2007

Project #8: "Mapping a Life"

Overview:

While it's common to describe one's life as a journey, creating a map as a metaphorical portrayal of a life is an interesting way to chart personal information and engage students who are more visually oriented. In this pop-up map book, life's challenges, struggles, pleasures, and surprises are depicted in the language and graphics of cartography (i.e. crossroads, bridges, deserts, mountains, canyons, etc.). While the form and the content are developed simultaneously, we'll start with making the book form, so that students can begin to plan where they want to place the features they choose to represent on the map.

"Mapping a Life" gives students a chance to learn the concept of a controlling image or metaphor. A controlling image, or metaphor, is defined as "an image that dominates, controls, unifies, and often gives impulse to a poem. The poem implicitly or explicitly continually refers to the controlling image."[6] In this project, students are asked to write autobiographical pieces which describe their own lives using the language of geography, geology and travel. You may want to introduce the concept of controlling image or controlling metaphor at the outset.

Pop-up map book, closed.

Pop-up map book, open.

Materials:

- one sheet of drawing paper, 11 × 11″
- ruler
- pencil
- bone folder
- cardstock or thick art paper (e.g. Canson Mi-tientes) for cover, 13 × 5¼″
- 1/8″ ribbon, 32″ long
- hole punch, any shape, at least 1/8″ in diameter
- gluestick
- art materials (paint, colored pencils, markers, etc.) for drawing the map
- extra finepoint permanent markers for lettering on the map (e.g. Pigma Micron or Zig Millennium)
- templates on pages 155-160

Procedure:

1. Make a photocopy of the template for each student, so that they can practice the folds and start to plan where they want to put the features of their maps.
2. Using this mock-up as a guide, have them sketch their maps on "good" paper, and then add surfacing techniques, paint, collage, illustration, or other visual details of the map features. Writing on the map should be done with a permanent (waterproof) fine marker.
3. Rather than creasing the original artwork, it's a good idea to have a color copy made. It will be easier to fold the copy, since any collaged parts will make the map too bulky to

[6] Myers & Simms, *The Longman Dictionary of Poetic Terms*

fold, or will just fall off. You might suggest making more than one color copy, in case the folding doesn't go well the first time.

4. Take the cardstock and fold in half, horizontally, so that it is 6½ × 5¼″.
5. From the folded edge, measure in 5½″ on both sides of the cover, score, and fold the for edges into the cover.
6. At the midpoint of the height of the cover (2 ⅝"), mark each foredge and the spine fold.
7. With the folded-in flaps in place, punch holes at the foredge of the front and back covers, where marked.
8. Fold the cover closed and, aligned with the mark you made on the spine, punch a hole through the front and back covers about 1″ in from the spine edge (see illustration at left).

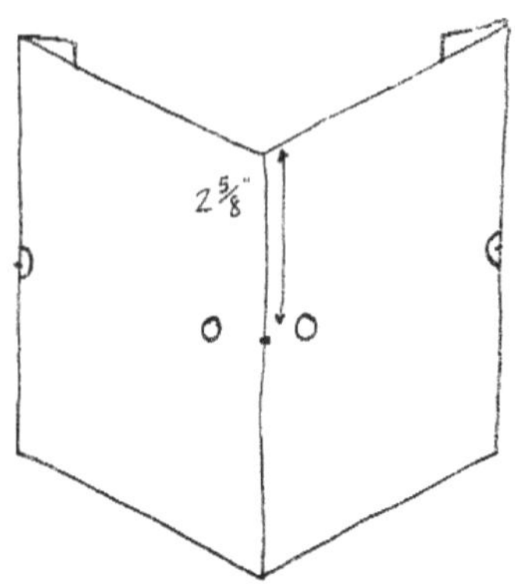

Cover for map book (step 8)

9. Insert the ribbon through the hole at the front foredge, through the inside of the cover and out the next hole, around the outside of the spine, back into the cover through the next hole, and out again through the hole at the back foredge. Even up the ends of the ribbon. Tuck the flaps in, and tack them down over the ribbon with gluestick.
10. Once the map is folded according to the template, it will fit within the covers, and should be glued in.

Warming Up:

There are dozens of ways to get students thinking in metaphoric terms. Some of my favorites include the following:

- List colors on the board. Ask students to tell you how each color sounds, smells, feels, and tastes. Encourage students to stay away from the obvious choices (red sounds like a fire truck), and go for fresher images (red sounds like a wrestler's roar when he downs his opponent). The point is the same: red is loud, but the second student has found a fresher figurative way of saying that.
- Hold up common objects and ask students to name something which is like that object in not so obvious ways. (A blackboard eraser is like an ice cream sandwich in color,

shape and dimension but not use. A mouse is like a storm cloud in color and perhaps in having soft outlines.) Do this with several objects.

- Share a favorite figure of speech and ask students to come up with a metaphor for its obverse. A second grader in one of my classes wrote, “The rain came down like a cemetery.” Most students assume this is a gloomy rain. Ask them to find language for the kind of rainy day in the summer when they might play in the puddles or see a rainbow.
- Look at magazines, and particularly at the language used in advertising. Ads often promote a product by linking it, directly or indirectly, with a feeling, accomplishment or desirable other product. See if students can identify how the language of sexual attraction or financial power is used to sell, for instance, a car.

This project provides a great opportunity to discuss the concept of a cliché. A cliché is a tired bit of figurative language. One way to sensitize students to overused phrases and figures of speech is to ask them to write an “anti-cliché” list poem. Write on the board a number of topics the descriptions of which often become cliché ridden. A few that come to mind include:

- Christmas (with its chestnuts on the open fire)
- Babies (little angels)
- War (honor, or blood and guts)
- Love (hearts beating as one)
- Sunset (orange balls lighting a sky)
- Bad weather (dark and stormy nights)

Ask students to come up with a list of images that could be associated with each of these topics. The task is to find images that are not common and overused. This can be a difficult assignment but can also generate much laughter when done in small groups.

You may want to warm up for this project more directly. Go through maps, atlases, geography and geology books. In the Appendix (where you found the template) is a list of “mappish” words as well as examples of generally recognized map symbols. Have students create a glossary of mapping language.

Ideas for an Autobiographical Map

List turning points in your life and then put these on a "roadmap" rather than on a time-line. For example, make highs go uphill and lows go downhill, show u-turns where something started one way and then reversed and detours when unexpected changes occur. Here's a list of transitional points a student might list that could be charted:

- Beginning: date and place of birth
- First school experience
- Changes of schools, graduations (including nursery on up)
- Births of younger siblings
- Learning new skills (e.g. riding a bike, musical instrument, driving, swimming)
- Getting a pet
- Death of a pet
- Death in the family
- Making a new friend
- Friend moving away
- New home/moving for student
- Parental divorce, remarriage, blending families
- Travel to far away places or nearby favorites

Have a discussion about what some of the terms could represent, and how the terminology could be applied to represent the ups and downs (in itself a figurative term for their experiences!) of their lives.

Creating Text:

You may want to have students make a rough time-line indicating high and low points in their lives. Each student should identify the theme of his or her journey. What does he want the reader to know about his life and experiences? How can this information and the feeling attending the experience be communicated using map language and symbol? Loss of a favorite grandparent may be represented by a cliff, a valley or a dark forest. A first love might be a winding or bumpy road.

Students can write out phrases to be included on the map. You may want them to create the text by cutting and collaging words and phrases from magazines, newspapers or even from old maps. In any case, students should move text around before deciding on a final form for their maps.

Alternative Applications:

Another option for this map book is to have students chart the life of a fictional or historical character.

You may want to collect all the students' maps, make a color photocopy of each before they are folded, and bind them together in an album format to make a class atlas.

Admittedly, the origami-like folds of this pop-up map might be beyond some students' abilities. A flat folded map in a cover might be a more familiar and accessible alternative for students who find the complicated folds too difficult. An alternative map fold diagram and directions are included with the templates in Chapter 10. An even simpler map form follows.

Materials:

- 1 sheet of paper 11 × 17″
- 1 sheet of cardstock, 11 × 5 ¾″

Procedure:

1. Hold paper horizontally and fold in half. Fold each half in half, so that you now have 4 panels.

2. Alternate the folds so that it is accordion-folded. You now have a folded sheet that is 4¼ × 11″. Fold the accordion in half so that it's now 4¼ × 5½″.
3. From each short side of the cardstock, measure in 4 ½″, mark, score, and fold. This leaves a ⅛″ spine to accommodate the bulk of the folded map.
4. Glue the back of the top half of the last panel of the map into the inside back cover. Your covered map is complete!

Project #9: A Collaborative Album

Overview:

Collaborative writing is a very old literary tradition. For centuries, linked verse was a major form of Japanese poetry. Similarly, poets wrote together in ancient China. Any kind of poem or story can be written collaboratively. This project is content driven and introduces many ways that students can work together on a theme. It also offers an opportunity for teachers to focus on the notions of sequencing and editioning an artist book. A stab-bound hardcover album that collects a class writing project will be created and can be left as a legacy to the school. Students acquire the skills to make personal albums while learning to make collaborative artistic choices.

Warming Up:

To get your students into the spirit of collaboration, you may want to play a group word game. Charades, Pictionary and team Hang Man all require students to work together with language and images. You might want to have the class create a group story using Mad Libs.

You can have a group create a silly story by having one student start the story with a sentence on the top of a sheet of paper. The paper is folded to conceal the sentence and then passed to the next student who adds a sentence, conceals this second sentence, and passes the paper on to a third student. Have students work in groups of five or six. When the last student has added a sentence, the paper is unfolded and the story read aloud to the group.

Collaborative Wishes Poem

Write a line (or two or three) starting with "I wish." Include a color and number in the line. (This was my particular direction; the teacher can make this as complicated as she/he wants—direct students to include a foreign country, a date, a certain number of syllables—however one wants to design this, it works.)

After the lines are written on file cards, the group decides an effective order for the lines and comes up with a title.

The following was pulled from 2nd and 3rd graders at a variety of different schools.

Wishes by the Numbers

I wish I had one soft, brown puppy.
I wish I had two blue eyes instead of gray ones.
I wish I was ten feet tall and could reach the white net with one hand.
I wish I had magic green sneakers and could jump a hundred feet up.
I wish I was eighteen and had a pink prom gown like my sister does.
I wish my three year old brother didn't spill red juice every morning.
I wish the tree by my house grew a hundred purple jelly beans.
I wish I could fly with my two large, red-feathered wings.
I wish the ground was covered in soft green grass instead of being
blanketed by a thousand white flakes of snow.
I wish the rain would stop and leave one big all color rainbow in the sky.

Many poem forms lend themselves well to group collaborations. The "It's About" form introduced earlier (see page 95) is one such poem. Wishes, in which every student contributes one line that begins "I wish" and concludes with a line that includes a common element (e.g., a color, a month, a food), make good group poems. Have the class write a collaborative poem about a color. This can be a type of list poem: name all of the associations with, for instance, red. Any list poem can be written as a group activity.

When artists collaborate, the end product is influenced by all the many parts and becomes its own whole, a reflection of every artist participating

The point to underscore with your students is that when artists collaborate, the end product is influenced by all the many parts and becomes its own whole, a reflection of every artist participating.

Content:

First choose a theme or subject for your album. Collaborative albums can be:

- Family recipes contributed by each student prefaced by the significance of the recipe
- Family stories or adages
- A personal memory of a particular category of experience (e.g., vacation, first days of school, travel, pets etc.)
- Memories of experiences the class shared
- Autobiographical sketches of each student
- School history collected by the students
- Descriptions of personal favorite places
- Individual testimonials to be left as a memento for the school

Once the group has defined the subject of the album and set parameters for the material to be included, individual students will create physical environments for their words and the text for their individual pages. When trying to decide what text to put on which page, it's useful to write out individual lines of a poem on Post-it® Notes and distribute them throughout the unbound sheets. When the text for each page is determined, students can use tracing paper to find the best placement of the words within the environment created by paper surfacing.

Depending on the budget, available materials, deadline, and any other limitations on project production, each student may be asked to produce one page or several pages.

After the album pages have been created and the cover made, and before the final project is assembled, students should work together to decide the order of the individual pages. Underscore that the "whole is greater than the parts." When poets, short story writers, or anthology editors put together a collection of work by one or more authors, they are guided by this: What comes before and after each page will effect how each individual page is read.

If students have created several pages, they may want to first work on creating a sequence of their own pages and then work with the class to create a sequence for the whole album. Have students read each other's work in round-robin groups and then discuss reasons for ordering pages in particular ways. What should be first? What page would make a good end note? Decide whether the album will have a forward or acknowledgments and if so, students can decide collaboratively what should go on these pages. You will find that students need to work and rework order. Discuss how each ordering of pages effects the tone, flow, feel of the book. You may want to show your students anthologies that you feel work well (or poorly) for some reason.

This project provides an opportunity for teachers to underscore the importance of the revision process in creating art, that revision is a process of "re-seeing" rather than just editing and cleaning up a work in progress.

Materials:

- 2 boards, 9 × 11″
- 2 boards, 9 × 1″
- 2 pieces of bookcloth, 3 × 10½″
- 2 pieces of bookcloth, 2¼ × 8¾″
- 2 pieces covering paper, 11 × 10½″
- 2 pieces covering paper, 9¾ × 8¾″
- paper for pages, 8¾ × 11½″ (cut down from 9 × 12″)

Procedure:

The procedure for making covers and binding this type of album is described in Chapter 6. Although the binding can be sewn as a stab-bound album, it's easier and more efficient in this case to use posts & screws so that additional sheets can be added.

Alternative Applications:

If students individually create a series of pages (four or more), these can be photocopied and bound alone with a soft cover stab bound stitch as described in Chapter 6.

Project #10: Foreign Correspondence

Overview:

Travel journals, on-the-road memoirs, pilgrimage accounts, letters from a distant land: there is a long history of books that recount personal adventure and transformation while away from home. This project asks students to imagine a voyage to an actual or invented place and to use the artifacts of travel—tickets, schedules, maps, postcards, travel agency ads, foreign currency, stamps, photos, letters on hotel stationery, receipts, etc.—to create an experience in which being an alien, away from the familiar, elicits personal reflection and recognition. This journey, presented as an external experience, is all about the internal adventure of discovering one's own frontiers and boundaries.

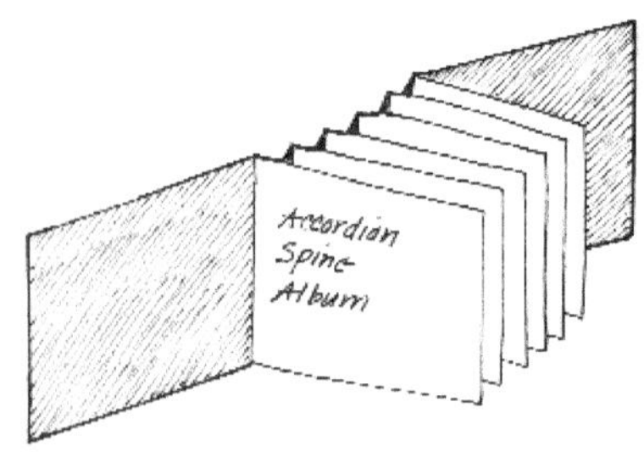

The writing portion of this project introduces the ideas of vignettes and sequencing of vignettes to create dramatic tension in a narrative. A vignette is a verbal snapshot, a short piece of writing that illuminates one scene or moment. Students will be asked to write many verbal snapshots related to their thematic journey and then create a sequence with these pieces.

The form of the book is a simple accordion spine album that allows for interactive inclusions of various dimensions and provides a kind of scrap book format to which to respond. High school students especially would be inspired by the remarkable *Griffin & Sabine* trilogy[7] by Nick Bantock. In each book a mystery unfolds through personal correspondence that the reader removes from envelopes. Bantock's fabulous illustrations and imaginary postage stamps and maps together with the narration of an improbable plot will engage both visual and verbal students.

Warming Up:

Since this project asks students to imaginatively enter a scene, you might want to begin by having students write to postcards or photos of actual scenes. Have each student bring five picture

---

[7] *Griffin & Sabine, Sabine's Notebook, The Golden Mean*, by Nick Bantock. San Francisco: Chronicle Books, 1991, 1992, 1993

Postcard

Questions:

Imagine the inside of the house:

- Who lives there or is it empty?
- What kind of furniture is in the house?
- What are the people doing?
- Who is the person outside hanging up a sheet? What is she thinking about while she does this task? Is she talking to someone hidden by the house? Is she alone?
- Is she humming? What tune?
- What might be behind the hill which is behind the house?
- Where is this house?
- Who used to live here?
- Is the house haunted? Who haunts it?
- Do any animals or birds live in the trees or hills?
- What year is this?
- Where in the world is this set?

The backpack on the rocks would be a good one for older students. Some questions:

- Why is this backpack by itself on these rocks?
- Did someone lose it? Abandon it? Put it down for a moment?
- Who owns it? Describe the owner.
- Describe what he or she has been doing before the backpack got put down.
- What's inside the back-pack?

Another tactic:

Write in the voice of the backpack to answer the above questions and add in the backpack's feelings.

postcards or photos of scenery. Students should exchange pictures before writing. You might want students to "pool" cards in a pile on a table and then give each student the opportunity to select a scene (not their own) which "calls to" him.

Once each student has selected a picture, ask him to write about the card. Direct the students not to describe the scene, but to enter it. You might suggest that they write about the scene beneath the scene shown by answering such questions as

- Who lives in the house in the photo?
- What's unseen behind the mountain?
- Whose laundry hangs on the line?
- If you followed the road pictured, where would it lead you?

In short, if you could walk around *in* the scene, what or who might you see, hear and encounter? As a variation on the warm up, you could show slides of paintings of scenery and have students write to these paintings.

You can also prepare your students to write snapshots by introducing a short, evocative, descriptive poem that describes a place as a model. One of my favorites is "Nantucket," by William Carlos Williams.[8] Williams's poem evokes the peaceful, fresh feeling of the traveler to Nantucket simply by detailing the elements in one room. Read the poem with the class and ask students to name the feeling the poem evokes. What details create the feelings named? Once the students have considered the model, you might ask them to write their own "snapshot poem." Students should name a favorite place and list five or six concrete, sensory details that characterize this place. Encourage students to write as if they are seeing the place for the first time and ask them to try to select the details they believe would best communicate their reaction to the place in the fewest words.

Creating Text:

Students can begin creating text in response to real artifacts collected, (ticket stubs and receipts, photos, maps etc.). Some students will choose to enter this project by collecting artifacts of the journey they aim to depict in their books. These students

[8] *Sleeping on the Wing*, Kenneth Koch and Kate Farrell, page 137.

can be directed to sit with each artifact and write a paragraph or a series of lines about each piece collected. Students should not simply describe the appearance of each artifact, but consider its significance. Direct students to write about the show the ticket stub came from, the other passengers on the trains for which they hold schedules, the aloof clerk at the hotels from which they saved keys. In other words, you will be asking students to follow the idea developed in the post card warm up: don't just describe a scene but enter it imaginatively. Some of this imaginative entering of scene will involve physical description of place, but physical description should be only part of what is offered. Some pieces might be written in the form of letters to a friend. Other pieces might take the form of diary entries. Still other writing might take the form of lists: first aid items to buy for the trip, what animals were seen from the window of the train, even a list of people to whom to send postcards. Some pieces can take the form of direct observation while others reflect on the significance of a moment or place.

Students may want to begin by writing the vignettes directly from imagination and create or collect artifacts that illustrate the imagined journey once the moments have been depicted.

Whether writing precedes collection of artifacts or proceeds from it, the bits of writing will need to be ordered after all are written. The most obvious and pedestrian sequencing of written pieces would be to order the events chronologically. Encourage students to break with chronology. Have students write each of the vignettes (paragraphs or small poems) onto file cards. Let them shuffle their cards and read the pieces in random order, then reshuffle and reread. What order creates a sense of mystery or tension? What is the turning point moment of the journey? Is there a vignette that might hook a reader? This would make a good beginning point even if it is not the beginning of the journey. The turning point moment should go near, but not at, the end of the sequence.

In this case, the adage that the journey is more important than the destination applies not only to the content of the writing but also to the process by which it is put together.

Students should be encouraged to explore non-linear sequencing of their pieces. Quirky outcomes that create emotional resonance should be rewarded even if a logic to the sequence is not easy to articulate.

Materials:

- 2 boards, each 9″ × 7″
- 2 pieces of cover paper, each 10½″ × 8½″
- 2 pieces of liner paper (can be the same as cover paper), each 8½″ × 6″
- cardstock for accordion spine, 11″ × 7″ (with grain running parallel to the 7″ sides)
- cardstock for pages, 8½″ × 7″ (9 or 10 sheets)
- bookbinding Kit
- envelopes
- paper for letters
- photo corners
- misc. papers & art supplies for making stamps, postcards, tickets, etc.
- ephemera from actual trips (maps, photos, schedules, etc.)

Procedure:

1. Cover each board with paper, using glue and mitering corners. Do not line the cover boards. Press the boards to prevent warping.
2. Fold the cardstock in half vertically (making sure that the grain runs parallel to the fold). Measure in 1″ from each short side of the cardstock, score, and fold. The distance between that fold and the center fold is 4½″. Measure and mark each half inch between these initial folds; score along those ½″ marks, and fold, accordion style.
3. Once the cardstock is folded into an accordion fold spine, glue the 1″ portions to the inside front and back covers, which have been pressed. Do not line the covers until the very end.
4. Pages can now be surfaced to create environments (Chapter 4), collaged, illustrated, or written on. This should be done before gluing the pages into the accordion spine. A few ideas about pages:
    - They don't all have to be the same color.
    - Ephemera and artifacts can be mounted onto pages with glue, tape, photo corners, inserted into slits cut into the page, or sewn in. Think of how scrap books are cobbled together.
    - Pockets can be added to contain items that you might not want to adhere to a page (e.g. feathers, foreign currency, or stamps).
    - Envelopes containing letters can be pasted onto a page face down so that the opening is accessible, or face up (so that it can be addressed and stamped) with the flap sealed and then the top slit open with a letter opener.
    - You can photocopy a portion of a map on one of the pages and use that as a background for text or image.

- Windows can be cut in some of the pages to reveal something on a subsequent page.

5. Once pages have been completed and sequenced, adhere each with a thin line of glue onto the mountain fold facing the front of the book. There will be enough folds to accommodate nine pages. If you want more pages, use a longer strip of cardstock for your accordion spine.
6. Finishing touches: line the inside front and back covers with your lining paper, covering the accordion spine attachment. Add a title bar on the cover and a colophon describing your materials and methods on the inside back cover. When you are completely finished, press the closed book under a weight.

"Late Bloomers," an accordion spine artist book by Meg Kennedy, text by Liz Abrams-Morley.

Alternative Applications:

Describe a trip to a specific place, real or fictional, that is being studied in social studies or literature classes. Students can collect real artifacts from that place (stamps, post cards, etc.) or create artifacts that might be found in a fictional place.

Rather than traveling through place, travel in time. Have students journey through a time period under study in history class and create vignettes and artifacts relevant to that historical period.

Create a poem sequence. Ask students to pick a destination/ place and then consider how they might write about the same place in a number of different ways. Each bit of writing can use a different poetic form or rhythmic structure. A classic model poem sequence is Wallace Stevens's "Thirteen Ways of Looking at a Blackbird."[9] Many poets write sequences about places or objects in the natural environment. The short poetry pieces should be ordered with a consideration to both the dramatic and rhythmic flow created by words and images.

[9] Kenneth Koch, *Rose Where Did You Get That Red?*

Project #11: Altered Books & Found Poetry

Overview:

Altered books and found poetry are visual and verbal equivalents. Both activities work with materials at hand, recycling and transforming someone else's work into something entirely new. In a way, it's a collaboration between the artist and the original author. Altered books and found poetry can be done together as one project or created as two separate projects

Book altered by Meg Kennedy.
left page: spray paint tie dye
right page: spatter paint with
masked-out words, window cut
through and to the next page

Altered books

Since we teach children not to deface books, this is a project that is better suited to older students, who will individually select a discarded, donated, or very inexpensive used book to alter with 2- and 3-dimensional techniques and materials. An altered book involves removing, gluing, and painting pages, collaging, rubber stamping, cutting windows, and even adding drawers. Students select a theme and produce a series of two-page spreads that incorporate many of the paper surfacing techniques that were described in Chapter 4. Text can be added to the resurfaced page or found on the page and highlighted to create a new message. This is a playful activity: encourage students to interact with the already existing visual and verbal environments found in their books, changing what's there to make it their own.

Found poetry

Found poetry is created when a piece of writing that was not intended as a poem, without changes in concept and without major reorganization, is laid out in a way that could be considered a poem. Often these are "wrested from a mundane domain ... and isolated so that it takes on an ironic, dramatic or multi-layered meaning."[10] Parts of newspaper or magazine articles, cooking directions on the sides of prepared food boxes, notes left by one's mother, legal documents—all have been used to create found poetry.

[10] Myers & Simms, *The Longman Dictionary of Poetic Terms*, p. 118.

The author of the found poem must decide on the poem's limits and be aware of the effect of the line break on both the meaning and rhythm of the work. This project offers an opportunity to sensitize students to the poem as a visual piece.

Warming Up:

I often start a discussion of poetry layout by pointing out the ways in which a poem's visual placement on the page is a kind of scaffolding or architecture for the ideas it contains. Have students warm up their scaffold-making brains. I tell the class that for the moment we are an architectural firm being asked to design a building. First students create a client, a family of a given size, for instance, with pets, multiple generations and varied medical and personal needs. What sort of house might we create for this family?

Now change the client by reducing the number of people, letting go the pets, downsizing the variability of needs, and discuss how the architectural recommendation will change.

Similarly, a poem about a leisurely day at the beach might "want" to be laid out in long and languid lines, whereas a poem about shopping in Manhattan might burst out in small phrases that are laid out unevenly over the page. The form should "contain" the meaning in some deliberate way.

Much has been written about how poets choose where to break lines. When a poem is written in a given form, the line contains a predetermined number of beats that create a predetermined rhythm. Free verse does not offer up a neat set of rules for breaking lines. What you as a teacher will want to know is that the line break effects both the rhythm and meaning of a line.

Found Poems

[selected and edited from a paragraph in an Amtrak magazine (Arrive Magazine, July/August 2007, p. 18)]

How to Fold Shoes

Packing a Suitcase. There are three types–
rollers
folders
crammers.
And there are theories
about wrinkles
and space saving
but no one knows
what to do with
shoes.
Shoes.
They just sit there
At the bottom
taking up space.

– Liz Abrams-Morley

Found Poem

[selected and rearranged from a chemistry book, The Periodic Kingdom, by P.W. Atkins, NY: Basic Books, 1995, pp. 41-42]

The Chemistry Between Us

A ray of light hits metal
and loose electrons
oscillate in harmony
with the radiation.

We see a mirror image:
a portrait of the ripples
in the electron sea.

–Meg Kennedy

One of my favorite line break warm up exercises is described by Joseph Tsujimoto in his book *Teaching Poetry to Adolescents*.[11] Students are asked to arrange a group of words (written on the board as a block of prose) into a form that looks like a poem. No words are to be added or deleted and the order of the words should not be altered. Tsujimoto's example includes the sentence, "My brother is an animal lover sometimes hater." A line break indicates a pause in the reading of the line, a breath. Note how the rhythm of the poem changes when the lines each contain two words:

My brother
is an
animal lover
sometimes hater.

Notice how meaning differs between the opening line of the student who writes: "My brother is an animal lover" as opposed to the student who begins her poem "My brother is an animal."[12]

You can create any number of such lines of your own and have students try dividing them. Discuss the effect of variations as a group.

Annie Dillard has published an entire collection of found poems in her book *Mornings Like This*.[13] You may want to read some of this book with your class when you begin this project.

Creating Text:

Students can create found poetry from textbooks, newspapers, cookbooks, road signs, bumper stickers; the possibilities are endless. You can ask your students to eavesdrop on conversation in a cafe or on a bus and jot down bits of dialogue which can be cobbled into a found poem.

Encourage play with this assignment. Write words that do not relate directly to music (but have a musical sound) directly onto staff paper. Write directly onto the newspaper or alter the newspaper by blacking out parts of articles and creating a new text from the words left revealed. Clip phrases from a magazine

[11] Joseph Tsujimoto, *Teaching Poetry to Adolescents*
[12] Ibid.
[13] Annie Dillard, *Mornings Like This*

and arrange them onto a found poem poster. See what happens when the words are laid out in a new order.

Found poems can be "found" in the altered books your students make. Words in the text are concealed or revealed through windows to multiple pages. A found poem can be collaged into an altered book.

Procedure:

There is no right or wrong way to alter a book, and since it's a hot topic on the crafts circuit these days, there are numerous books that describe various techniques. Students should choose a book that appeals to them, either in terms of appearance or topic. An altered book can be a form of visual journaling in which each spread of pages provides a new place to begin, or you can identify a theme and develop it throughout the volume selecting words from the original book and adding your own to support the subject chosen. A third option is to use random words from the original text to construct a new narrative that is developed throughout the book. Not all pages will be worked on; students should aim for 10-12 double-page spreads, so that the project has some hope of being completed. It's a good idea to require students to use at least 4 or 5 of the paper surfacing techniques so that the environments created have variety. Here are a few ways to alter a book:

1. Outline certain words on the page that speak to you, and paint out the rest.
2. Collage images (photos, magazine pictures, your own drawings) onto pages and select words that speak to the images, obscuring the rest with paint, marker, crayon, etc.
3. Cut or tear out a page 1″ from the fold, leaving a flap on which a substitute page of your own devising can be glued.
4. Fold in a corner or foredge of a page and glue down to create a pocket into which an artifact or message can be inserted. The glued attachment can also be sewn with decorative threads to add texture and interest.
5. Paste several pages together to make one thick page and cut a window through it. Use a new blade in your X-Acto® knife and work over a cutting mat or thick cardboard so as

Materials:

- a used hardcover book*
- Basic Bookbinding Kit
- X-Acto® knife and extra blades
- acrylic medium (gloss or matte) + brush
- materials for individual paper surfacing techniques
- collage materials
- optional: rubber stamps and stamp pads, fancy edged scissors, punches, decorative fibers and other embellishments

* Check thrift shops, flea markets, yard sales, and used book stores. Our local library sells donated books for $1/bag: another good source. Make sure the book is firmly bound and does not contain old yellowed pages, which will disintegrate as you work on them.

Book altered by Meg Kennedy. Left page shows selected text and collaged images that relate to the text; right page shows painted image that relates to the text selected

not to cut through subsequent pages. On the page following the thick windowed page, adhere an object that relates with your theme (e.g. a charm, a key, a button, etc.). The thickness of the windowed page will allow 3D additions without making the book bulge open.

Book altered by Meg Kennedy. Left page painted, right page shows selected text and found poetry strung across a window out into the page(steps 1 & 2)

6. Punch holes around the edge of several pages and lace thread, ribbon, yarn through the holes. Charms, beads, shells, and other embellishments can be added to the fiber lacings. Insist on relevancy, however. We're not "decorating" the book, each addition should further the focus of the book.
7. Either at the front or the back of the book (you need a hard cover to support this), you can construct a shadow box into which a dimensional assemblage can be added. Take a section of the book, at least a ½″ thickness, and brush acrylic medium around the edges of the pages. This will adhere them together. With a new blade in your knife, cut an opening through the entire thickness, a little at a time. If the edges of your opening are rough, you can sand them or smooth irregularities with an emery board. Brush acrylic medium along the cut edges to adhere the center of these pages together. Surface the top page as desired and glue the section down onto the front or back cover. Your shadow box assemblage is glued to the cover.

Book altered by Meg Kennedy. Left page shows collage; right page shows collage plus selected text.

8. With an X-Acto® knife, cut straight or wavy lines horizontally down a page (over a cutting mat), leaving an inch uncut around the edges. Through these slits, weave strips of paper and fiber.
9. Attach an envelope that contains a letter, photo, or artifact (e.g. a feather) to a page. This invitation to interact with the book is exactly what artists' books are all about.
10. A small drawer can be added to the text block by using a matchbox. Adhere a stack of pages the thickness of the matchbox by painting around the edges with acrylic medium. When the pages are dry, trace the shape of the matchbox on the top page, flush up against the edge from which the drawer will extend. With a new blade in your knife, cut away the paper; you can sand the opening if it is ragged. Brush acrylic medium along the edges you have just

cut to adhere the block of paper. Apply glue to the matchbox and attach a bead, button, or extension to the end of the "drawer" so that you can pull it out. Once the matchbox is secured in the space you have cut, glue the next page over the top to hide all the cutting. Place a treasure in the drawer.

Tips:

Don't use extremely wet techniques right in the book; the moisture will cockle all of the pages. If you want to incorporate suminigashi marbling or pastepaper, execute these techniques on other sheets of paper which you can add to the book once they are dry.

Project #12: Free-Form Exploration

Overview:

If your students are brimming with ideas, resistant to authority, and independent in nature and work habits, they will love this assignment. This is the least directed, and therefore, in some ways, the most sophisticated project. In doing their own free-form exploration, students will employ skills they have attained while making earlier projects, and will draw from within themselves to create a personal statement in artist book form. In this non-linear, non-traditional volume, content and form are created simultaneously.

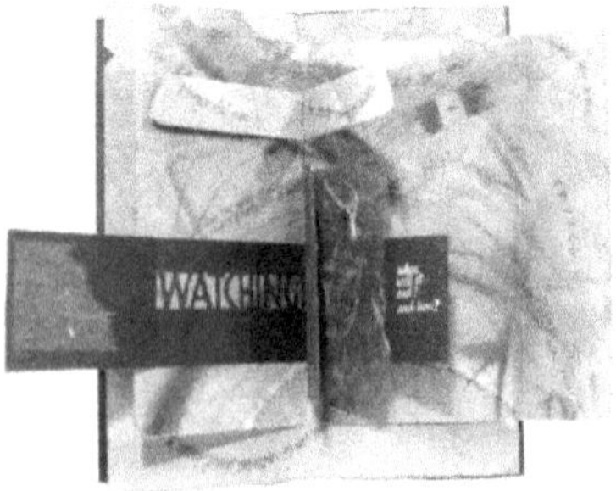

In order to get students to rethink the notion of book format, one requirement should be that they combine at least 2 of the forms that have been introduced. For example, an accordion fold book with signatures sewn into some or all of the valley folds would be a different setting for text than a pamphlet with a centerfold section of accordion-folded pages. The other requirement is the use of at least three paper surfacing techniques. The materials needed will be determined by the individual artist, as will the specific directions for constructing a non-traditional or combination form.

"Darkness"
by Meg Kennedy, 1997

As a teacher, you may find that this is the most difficult project to assess as each student's selection of theme will dictate form and content. The end products are likely to vary quite a bit. We suggest that when assessing this project, the primary standard of judgment should be how well students express their themes visually and verbally. Did the student make an integrated statement relevant to the chosen theme?

Warming Up:

This project assumes you have had your students journaling throughout the year or for an extended period of time. If your students do not write in a journal regularly, have them spend five or ten minutes free writing several times over a period of a month before beginning this project.

Encourage students to record sayings, phrases, poems, lyrics, bumper sticker slogans, or any words that speak to them on a given day. Some students will even paste bits of language into their journals: significant fortunes from cookies, or their horoscopes clipped from the daily newspapers.

Creating Text and Form:

Students begin this project by reading through journal entries and identifying recurring themes in their own writings. You might suggest that students use a yellow highlighter to mark words or images that appear again and again, or to pull out phrases that seem to carry emotional resonance. From the highlighted portions of the journal, students will identify one theme for their own free-form book project.

In order to determine the shape, size, palette, and binding of their unique artist's book, students should refer back to the section on Making Choices in Chapter 3. It's a good idea to duplicate this list of questions and give a copy to each student, who will revisit the many options available, make choices, *and document the reasons for those choices*. Although we call this a "Free-form Exploration," it is not intended to be a chaotic mish-mash of random expression. That's what journaling can be. This activity is structured, but unlike previous projects, its structure is internally motivated: each artist is responsible for every variable in the book.

1. Find a theme
2. Make choices

3a. Objective theme:
- identify subjective feelings

3b. Subjective theme:
- clarify with objective examples

4. Make a model

Some students will want to start by making a model book and altering it as their text develops, adding windows, pockets, extensions to complement the words and images. Others will want to focus on content and develop the form of their book as a response to the words. Both strategies are correct. There are, however, ways to guide your students so as not to overwhelm them. Here are a few ideas:

- Determine the type of palette your theme dictates—cool/warm, light/dark, specific colors—and suggest at least one session of nothing but paper surfacing in that chosen palette so that each student will have a pile of papers from which to draw inspiration. A theme that expresses lightness or contentment will differ in color, texture, and form from one that focuses on sadness or fear. Nothing sidesteps "fear

Tuck a secret inside an envelope.

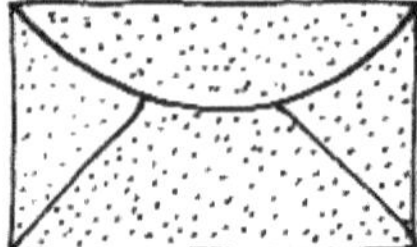

of white space" more effectively than a paper on which some environment has been created.

- If the student's theme is objective—going off to college, a beloved pet, my best friend, lacrosse—identify the subjective feelings associated with it. In the first instance, for example, "going off to college" might elicit excitement, fear, homesickness, bravado, confusion, and a host of other emotional responses. Have the student list these emotions and then portray them physically. Exuberant gestural strokes indicating excitement would contrast dramatically with scribbles indicating confusion. By nonrepresentational depiction of each emotion, students will start to determine the "look" of their pages.
- If the student's theme is subjective—love, anxiety, mourning, contentment—the same physical portrayal should be done, but this time looking for objective examples of such an emotion, in other words, looking for symbols and similes. From "Happiness is a warm puppy" to "Hope is the thing with feathers," such metaphors will help to shape the design of the book.
- Since journal entries often deal with self-discovery, secrets, and longings, students should think about the physical portrayal of concealing and revealing by adding doors to open, windows to peer through, flaps, extensions, and pockets as depositories for text or image. "A tangled web" can be shown with thread woven through an open portion of a page. "A dark secret" can be, well, dark, and hidden behind a series of increasingly smaller doors or within a pocket.
- The notion of merging or intersecting two elements can be portrayed by actually weaving strips of paper, fiber, sticks, etc. Two texts that relate in some way or that completely conflict can be written out on separate papers, cut apart into strips, and woven together to create a "fabric" that reveals bits of each text.
- A simple element that is repeated on every page or 2-page spread can be a useful device in tying together what might look like a chaotic structure. Such a design element can be

an embossed shaped, a collaged image, a bit of stitching, a swatch of color, or a simple line.

- Once some of the student's choices have been made, a model of the format is made out of scrap paper. See how the model works to stage the text and then start on the book itself.

Once the book form has been created, students should go back to their journals and copy out highlighted lines, words or phrases to use as text in their books. This text can be combined with supporting text drawn from readings, song lyrics, fortune cookies, even overheard dialogue. Students who have already been collecting supporting text may find this material in their journals. Others will look for outside sources of supporting text once they have identified their themes.

Before finalizing the text onto their pages, students should cover each page with sheer tracing paper or treated acetate and write out the words in the position that suits the page design. Experiment with the layout of words in the book. Remember how the architecture of the writing (line breaks, punctuation, capitalization, etc.) affects meaning. The layout of the words; the style of lettering; the size, shape,and weight of the paper; the palette of the book: all should be chosen with care and support the mood and theme intended.

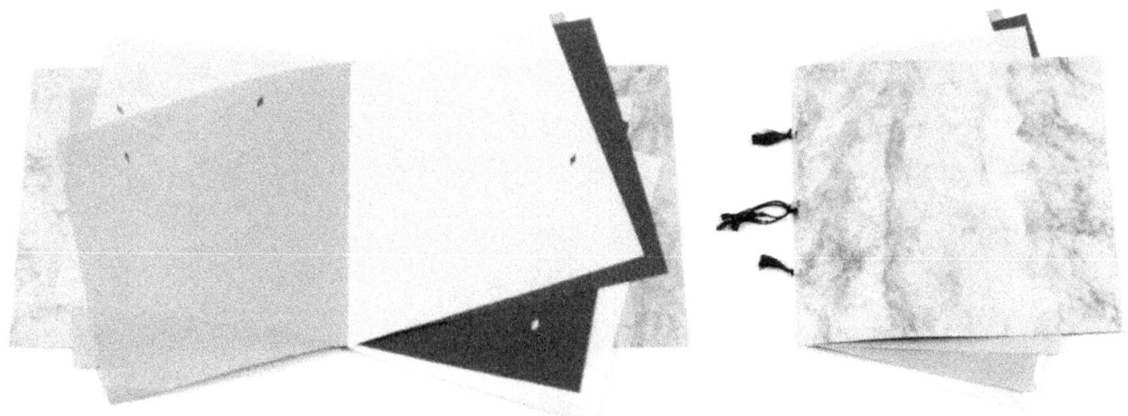

"Crooked Book," by Meg Kennedy open (left) and closed (right) .
Irregularly folded pages are sewn into the pamphlet form, suggesting pages that are "escaping" from within.

10 Appendix and Templates

This section contains vocabulary, diagrams, and templates to help you present the projects we have described. With the purchase of this book, you have the authors' permission to photocopy any of the pages in this chapter for distribution to your students. Some of it is general information and some is keyed directly to a particular chapter or project.

Here's what follows:

Anatomy of a Book (diagram) 150

Glossary of Basic Bookbinding Terms 151

Template for Marking Sewing Holes for a Pamphlet 152
for Chapter 6, p. 65

5-Hole Pamphlet Stitch 153
for Chapter 6, p. 65

Stab Binding Sewing diagram 154
for Chapter 6, p. 71

Pop-up Map Template 155
for Chapter 9, Project #8, p. 123

Alternative Map Fold template 156
for Chapter 9, Project #8, p. 123

Glossary of Map Terms & Synonyms 157
for Chapter 9, Project #8, p. 123

"Mappish" Words 158
for Chapter 9, Project #8, p. 123

Miscellaneous Lines & Graphics for Maps 159
for Chapter 9, Project #8, p. 123

Map Symbols 160
for Chapter 9, Project #8, p. 123

Some Altered Book Techniques 161
for Chapter 9, Project #11, p. 138

Anatomy of a Book

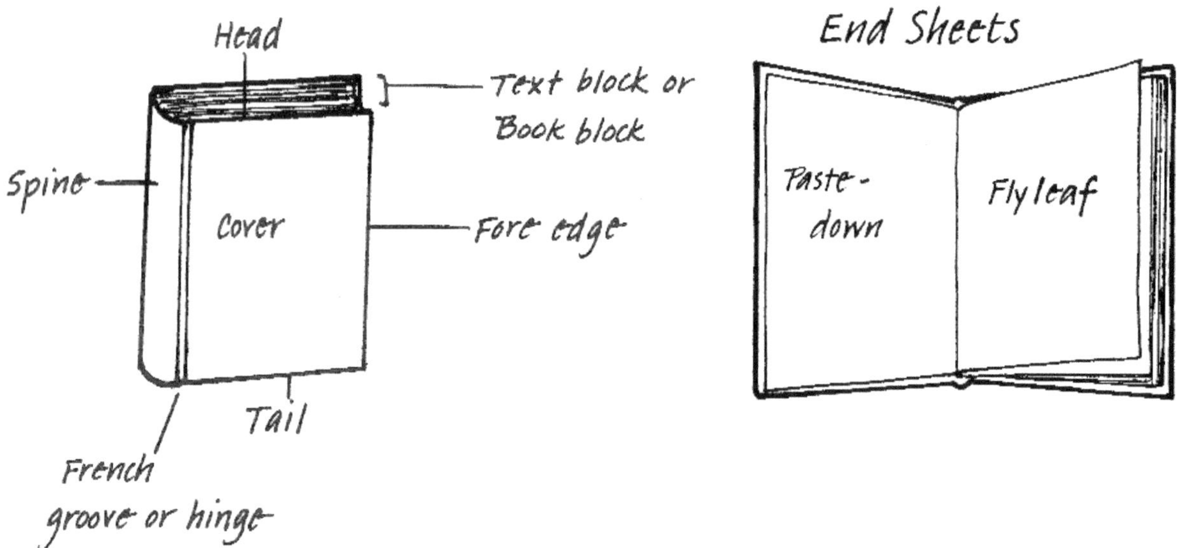

Colophon

The colophon is a statement at the end of a book containing facts relevant to its production, e.g. the printer, typeface, designer, paper, or reproduction methods. In artists' books, the colophon might describe the origin of the text, the materials and technique used, the number of copies, the purpose or inspiration for the book. It is also where the artist/author identifies herself, gives the date of completion, and signs the work. There is no set form for a colophon, but students should be expected to summarize and articulate their projects in a statement at the end of each book made. An example follows.

The text for this book was excerpted from Four Quartets, by T. S. Eliot (1943). The hand-lettering was done in ink on Arches hot press watercolor paper that was paste-painted and stenciled with oil pastel. The photographs were taken and hand-colored by Meg Kennedy. The book was made in response to questions about the passage of time and is a unique copy. Meg Kennedy, artist; 2008.

Selected Glossary of Basic Bookbinding Terms

Colophon Statement at the end of a book that describes its production

End Sheets First and last pages of the text block, sometimes decorative, often a contrasting color; first and last sheets are attached to the inside front and back covers and are called pastedowns. The sheets following and preceding the pastedowns are called flyleaves. (also called endpapers)

Folio One sheet or leaf folded in half (four pages)

Fore Edge Front edge of the book, where pages open

Gutter The valley or center fold of a folio or signature

Head Top edge of the book

Leaf Single sheet of paper

Page Oone side of the leaf, i.e. two pages equal one leaf

Sewing Stations Holes drilled or punched with an awl where pages will be sewn together

Signature A gathering of folios or folded sheets (also called section or quire)

Spine Back edge of the book, where pages are bound together

Tail Bottom edge of the book

Text Block All of the gathered folios (or signatures) and endsheets that are sewn or adhered together for placement in the cover

Template for Marking Sewing Holes for a Pamphlet

SINCE THE MEASUREMENTS FOR AN 8½″ SPINE ARE A LITTLE CHALLENGING FOR THE "RULER SHY," HERE IS A CHEATER RULER THAT CAN BE DUPLICATED FOR THE STUDENTS AND USED INSTEAD OF MEASURING.

FOR THE RECORD, THE HOLES ARE PIERCED AT THE FOLLOWING POINTS ALONG THE CENTERFOLD:
1″, 2-5/8″, 4-1/4″, 5-7/8″, 7-1/2″

5- HOLE PAMPHLET STITCH

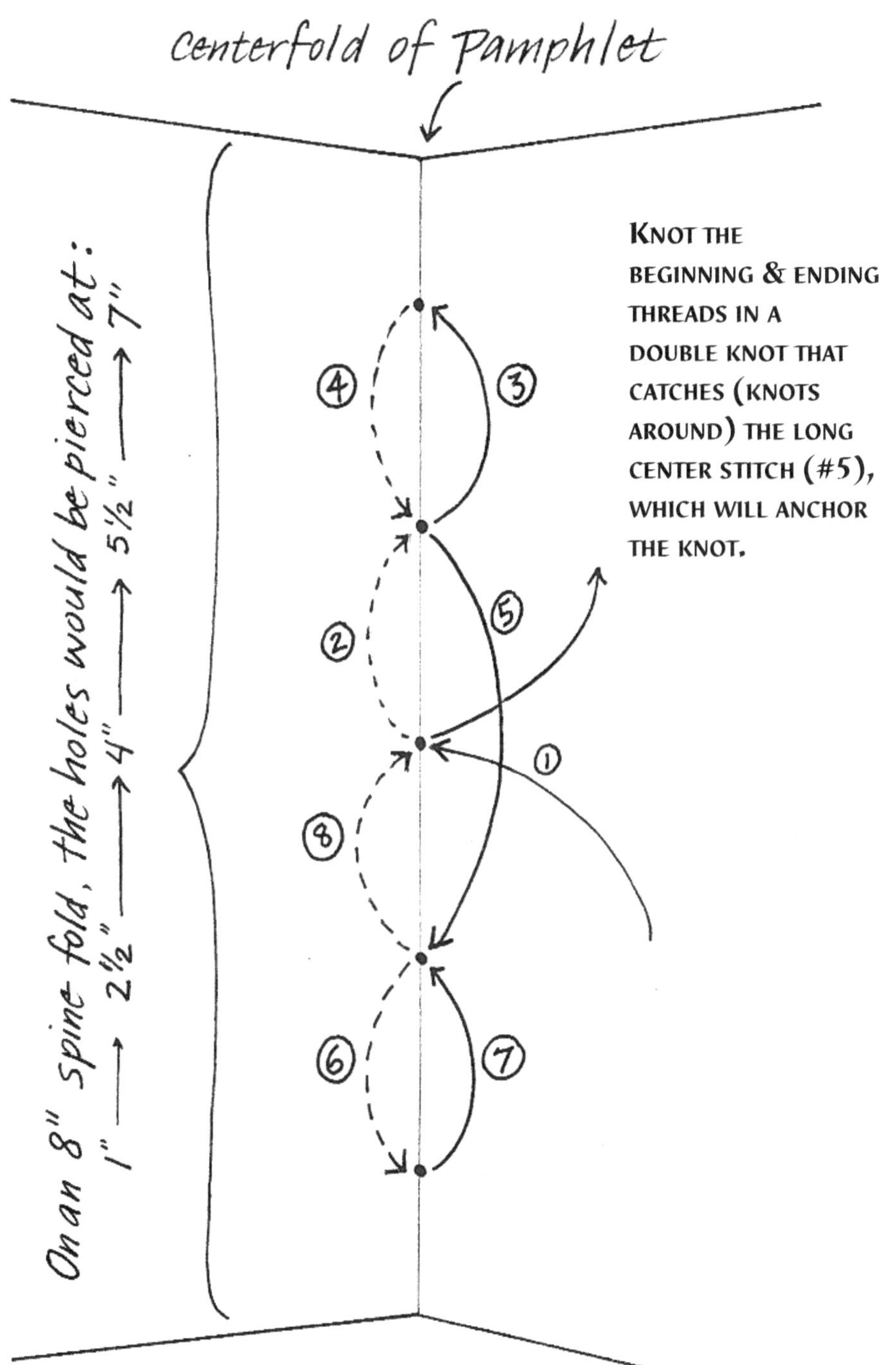

KNOT THE BEGINNING & ENDING THREADS IN A DOUBLE KNOT THAT CATCHES (KNOTS AROUND) THE LONG CENTER STITCH (#5), WHICH WILL ANCHOR THE KNOT.

Mark holes at 1" in from top & bottom of book, at the center, and midpoint between 1st & 2nd set of holes.

STAB BINDING

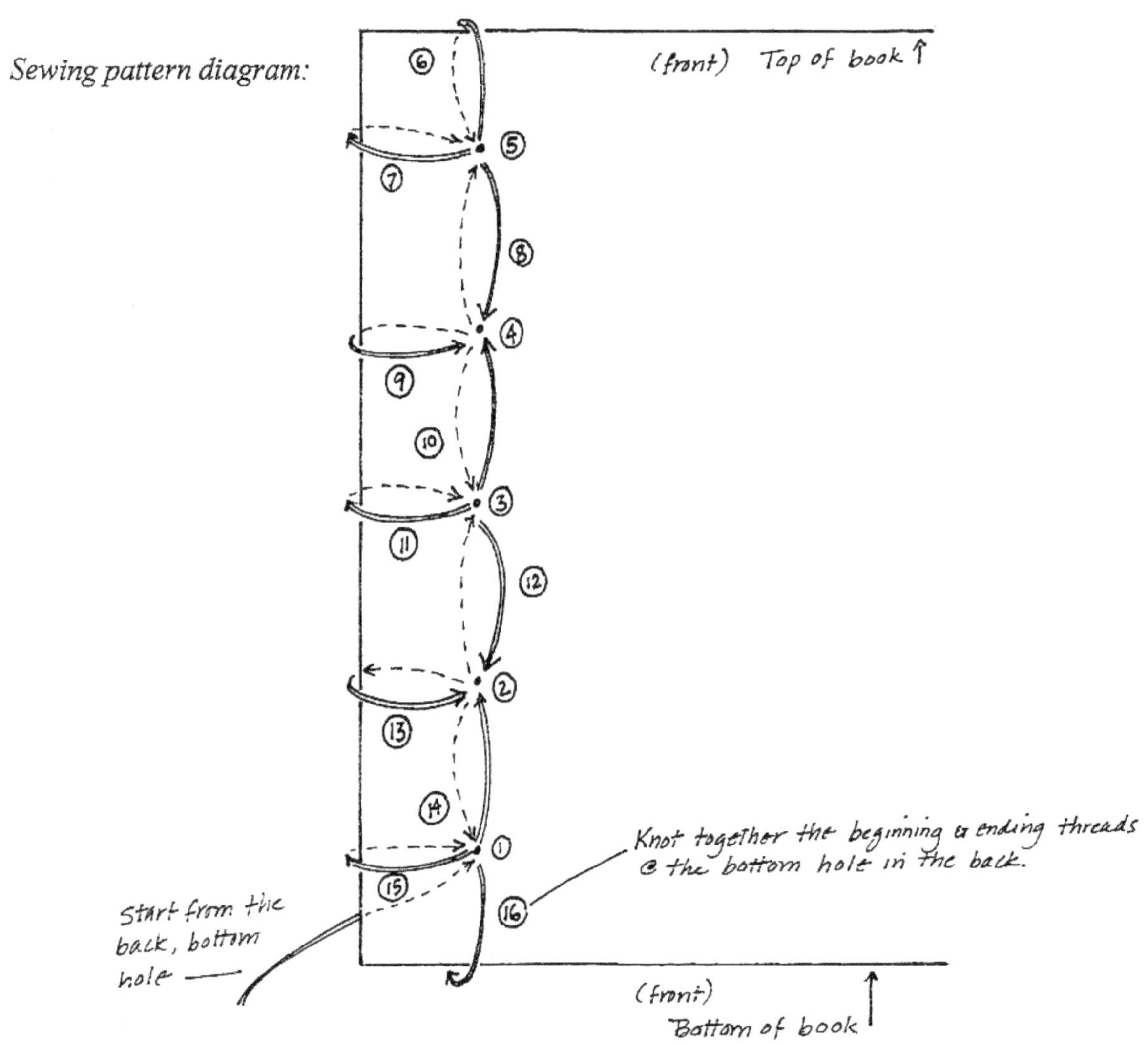

Pop-up Map template

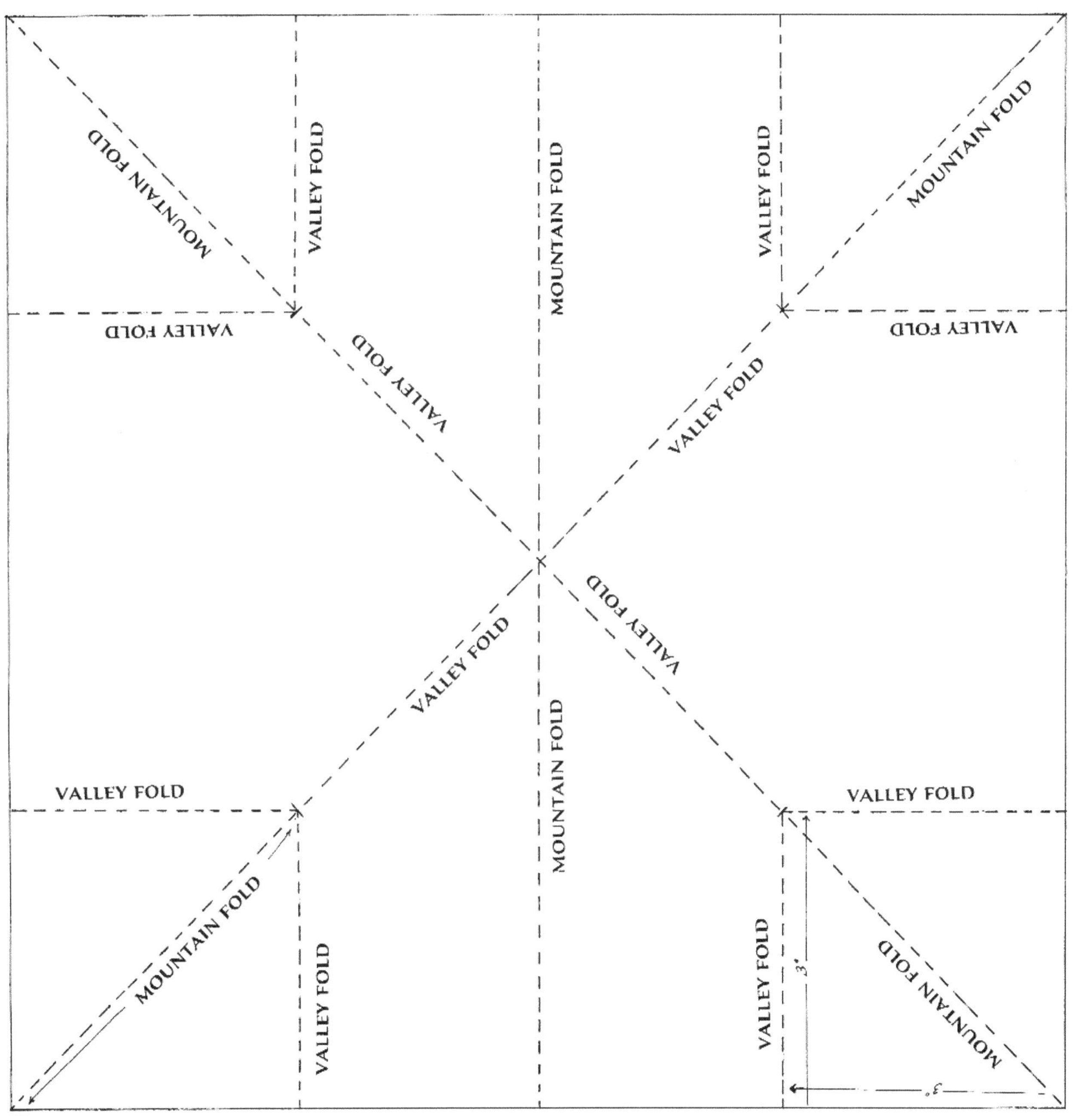

ALTERNATIVE MAP FOLD

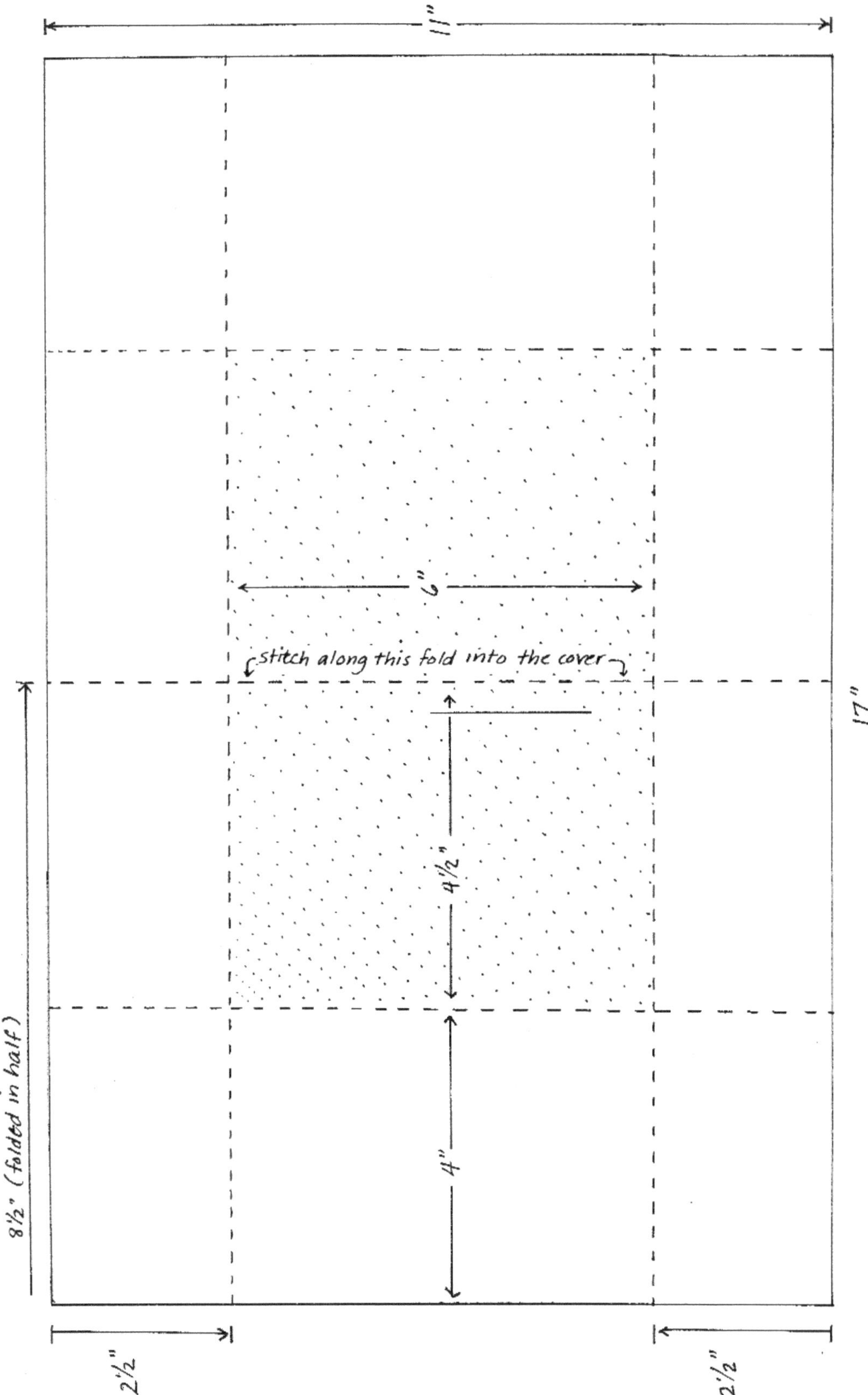

Folded map will be 4½"w x 6"h x ~¼-½" thick. Simple softcover is a cover-weight sheet 9½"w x 6¼"h, folded in half. Using a pamphlet stitch, sew the map (at centerfold) to the spine fold of the cover. The <u>back</u> of the central part of the map (shaded area) can be pasted to the insides of the cover.

Glossary of Map Terms & Synonyms

Map Terms

archipelago a group of islands

atoll a coral island consisting of a reef surrounding a lagoon

cataracts stretches of rapids and small waterfalls in rivers

delta fan-shaped area where a river empties into a larger body of water

fjord a narrow inlet of the sea between cliffs

headwaters the place where a river starts, the source

isthmus a narrow strip of land connecting two larger land areas

landlocked refers to areas that are entirely surrounded by land

levee a ridge of earth build to hold back flooding lakes and rivers

map a representation, drawing, portrayal, projection, plan, or diagram of a place.

oasis a fertile spot in the desert

orienteering using a map and compass to navigate your way along an unfamiliar course.

peninsula a portion of land connected to the mainland but jutting out into the water

savanna a large area of tropical grasslands covered in part with trees & shrubs

tributaries branches of rivers that join the main water course

tundra a vast treeless plain found in regions near the Arctic

Map Synonyms

city town, village, neighborhood

travel journey, trip, voyage, odyssey, course, movement, transit, progress, crossing, roam, ramble, wander, drift, stray, trek, tour, expedition, pilgrimage, excursion, outing, meander

"Mappish" Words

LAND WORDS

- archipelago
- atoll
- island
- isle
- isthmus
- peninsula
- reef
- sandbar
- borders
- boundaries

WATER WORDS

- bay
- cataract
- creek
- delta
- fjord
- harbor
- headwaters
- inlet
- lagoon
- lake
- ocean
- pond
- rapids
- river
- sea
- source
- spring
- tributaries
- waterfall

MAN-MADE STRUCTURE WORDS

- bridge
- campground
- dam
- levee
- park
- tunnel

TRANSPORTATION WORDS

- highway
- interstate highway
- public transit
- road
- route
- street
- trail

TERRAIN WORDS

- canyons
- caves
- desert
- forest
- geyser
- grasslands
- marsh
- mountains
- oasis
- pasture
- plains
- savanna
- shore
- swamp
- tundra
- valleys
- volcano

GENERAL GEOGRAPHIC WORDS

- compass
- latitude
- longitude
- mainland
- tropics

POPULATION CENTER WORDS

- city
- landlocked
- neighborhood
- seaport
- town
- village

TRAVEL WORDS

- travel
- course
- crossing
- drift
- excursion
- expedition
- journey
- meander
- movement
- navigate
- odyssey
- orienteering
- outing
- pilgrimage
- progress
- ramble
- roam
- stray
- tour
- transit
- trek
- trip
- voyage
- wander

MISCELLANEOUS LINES & GRAPHICS FOR MAPS

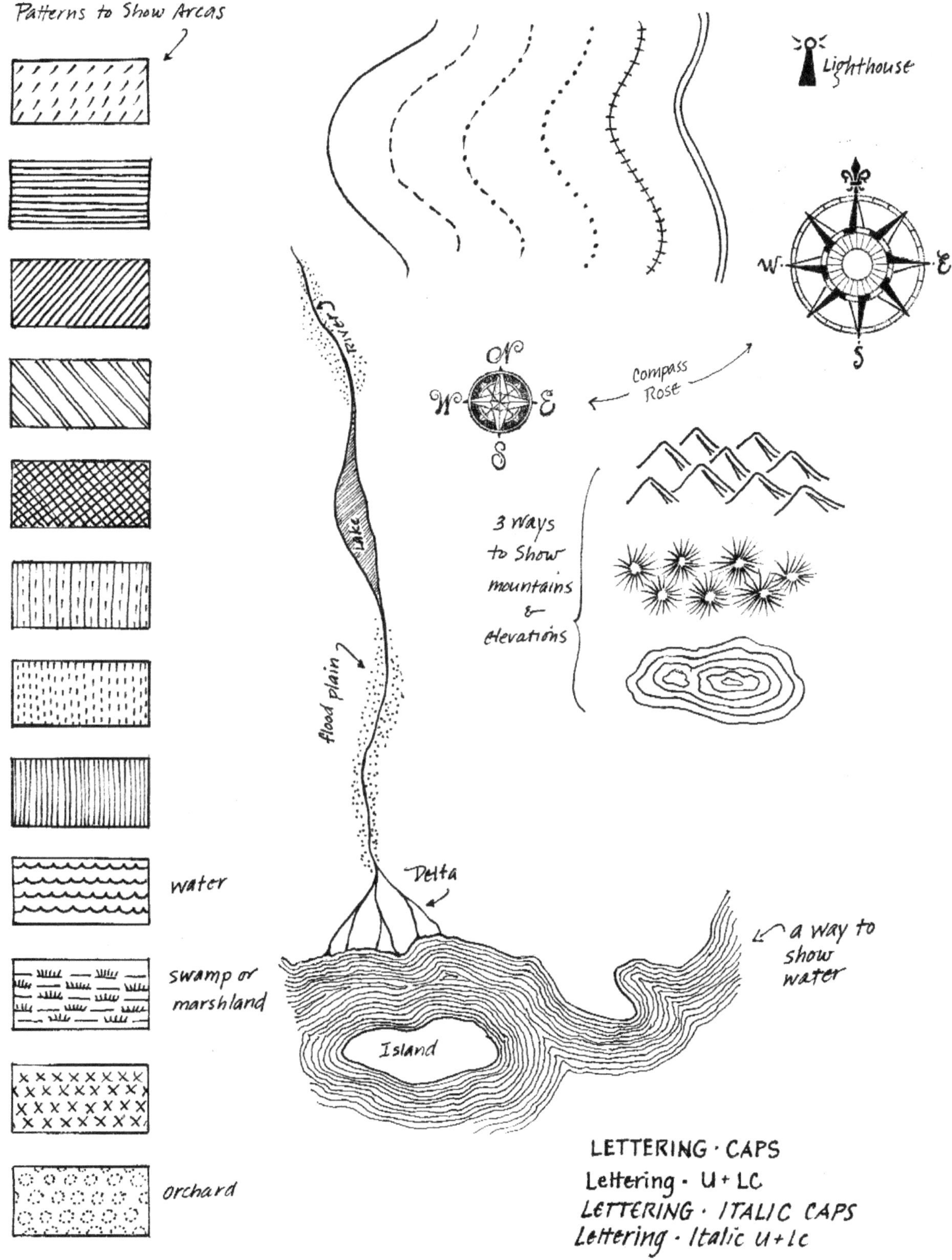

MAP SYMBOLS

Roads and Trails

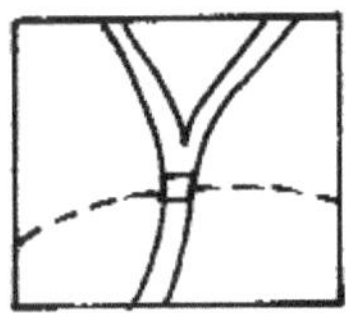
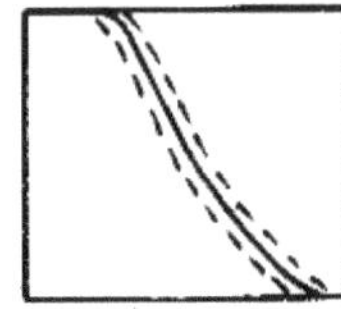
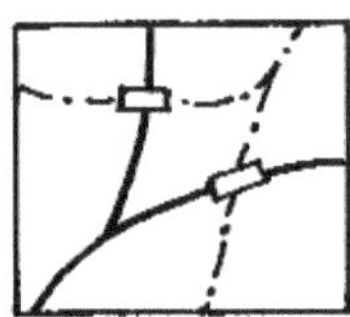

Bridge

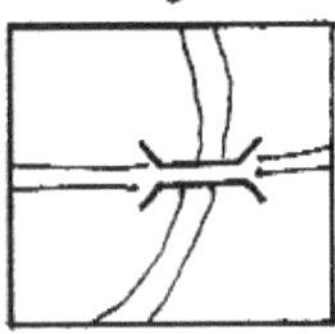

Railroad

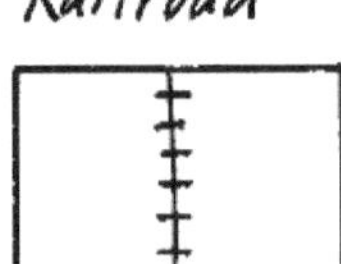

Buildings

School

Church

Cemetery

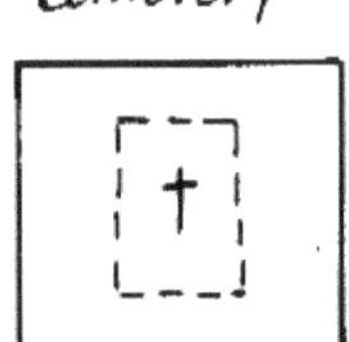

Lake

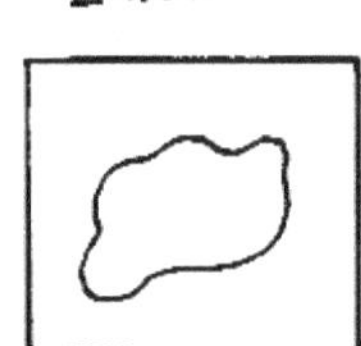

Ferry Crossing

Some Altered Book Techniques

1. Select text by highlighting the words you want to keep and masking out the rest (cross out, paint over, etc.).
2. Collage images onto pages.
3. Draw or paint images onto pages.
4. Write out a new text and substitute your page for one in the book.
5. Create pockets by folding in the corner(s) or fore edge of a page.
6. Cut windows or door into pages to reveal an addition on the next page.
7. Adhere several pages together to make one stronger, thicker section and cut a niche into it, to display a special object, artifact, coin, etc.
8. Add a fold-out map or a series of accordion pages that extend from the book.
9. Decorate or glue a new covering onto the cover to emphasize your chosen theme.
10. Adhere envelopes onto page, into which letters, instructions, secrets can be deposited so that the reader/viewer will interact with the book.
11. Cut a page apart and reassemble it in a different order to change the narrative and then reattach the altered page into the book (with tape, glue, sewing, etc.).
12. Design a symbol or image indicative of your theme, draw it onto a rubber eraser, and cut it out to make a rubber stamp that you can use throughout the altered book.
13. Add acetate overlays on certain pages so that you can add delicate objects (pressed flowers, leaves, feathers) that would be marred without protection. Attach the acetate overlay with double-stick tape, or punch holes around the edges and sew it onto the page.
14. Stencil onto the pages.
15. Lay one page over some texture (e.g. sandpaper) and do a texture rubbing (frottage) with colored pencil.
16. Replace pages in the book with ones that you have decorated with sumi marbling, chalk marbling, or bubble marbling and to which you've added text of your own.
17. Add a favorite quote on one page and on the following pages respond to it with words found in the book's text.
18. Weave strips of another text through the text on the page.
19. Spatter paint or sponge paint a 2-page spread in colors that create the environment of your theme and write over the color when it is dry.
20. Add some nature printing to your pages.

11 Resources

With the growing popularity in recent years of hand bookbinding, many art supply stores and arts & crafts chains have some materials and tools for making books. The following is a list of the suppliers that I use for book arts. There are many more outlets from which to choose; just search "bookbinding tools" on the internet and start shopping.

BOOKMAKERS, INC.

[a source for everything for making books]

8601 Rhode Island Avenue
College Park, MD 20740

www.bookmakerscatalog.com

phone: 301.345.7979
fax: 301.345.7373

email: bookmakers@earthlink.net

DICK BLICK ART MATERIALS

[general arts and crafts materials, including tools and quantity pricing on papers]

P.O. Box 1267
Galesburg, IL 61402

www.dickblick.com

phone: 800.828.4548
fax: 800.621.8293

HOLLANDER'S

[a source for everything for making books]

410 N. Fourth Avenue
Ann Arbor, MI 48104

www.hollanders.com

phone: 734.741.7531

email: info@hollanders.com

JOHN NEAL BOOKSELLER

[mail order calligraphy and book arts publications and supplies]

1833 Spring Garden Street
Greensboro, NC 27403

www.johnnealbooks.com

phone: 800.369.9598
fax: 336.272.9015

email: info@johnnealbook.com

NASCO ARTS & CRAFTS

[general arts and crafts materials, including tools and quantity pricing on papers; also they have the best prices on bone folders that I've seen anywhere]

901 Janesville Avenue
P.O. Box 901
Fort Atkinson, WI 53538

www.enasco.com/artsandcrafts/

phone: 800.558.9595
fax: 920.563.8296

email: info@enasco.com

PAPER & INK ARTS

[mail order calligraphy and book arts supplies and publications]

3 North Second Street
Woodsboro, MD 21798

www.paperinkarts.com

phone: 800.736.7772
fax: 888.736.7773
email: paperinkarts@aol.com

TALAS

[specializing in bookbinding and conservation]

330 Morgan Avenue
Brooklyn, NY 11211

www.talasonline.com

phone: 212.219.0770
FAX 212-219-0735

email: info@talasonline.com

12 Bibliography

Allen, Agnes. *The Story of the Book*. New York: Roy Publishers, 1967

Behn, Robin and Chase Twichell, editors. *The Practice of Poetry: Writing Exercises from Poets Who Teach*. New York: Harper Perennial, 1992.

Brazelton, Bev. *Altered Books Workshop*. Cincinnati: North Light Books, 2004.

Cecil, Nancy Lee. *For the Love of Language: Poetry for Every Learner*. Winnipeg: Peguis Publishers, 1994.

Collom, Jack. *Moving Windows: Evaluating the Poetry Children Write*. New York: Teachers & Writers Collaborative, 1985.

Collom, Jack and Sheryl Noethe. *Poetry Everywhere: Teaching Poetry Writing in School and in the Community*. New York: Teachers & Writers Collaborative, 1994.

Diehn, Gwen. *Making Books that Fly, Fold, Wrap, Hide, Pop Up, Twist, and Turn*. Asheville, NC: Lark Books, 1998

Dillard, Annie. *Mornings Like This*. NY: Harper Perennial, 1996.

Diringer, David. *The Book Before Printing: Ancient, Medieval and Oriental*. New York: Dover Publications, 1982

Dunning, Stephen M. Eaton and M. Glass, *For Poets: Poetry 2*, New York, NY: Scholastic Book Services, 1975

Feather, John. *A Dictionary of Book History*. New York: Oxford University Press, 1986

Gaylord, Susan Kapuscinski. *Multicultural Books to Make and Share*. New York: Scholastic Professional Books, 1994

Gensler, Kinereth and Nina Nyhart. *The Poetry Connection: An Anthology of Contemporary Poems with Ideas to Stimulate Children's Writing*. NY: Teachers & Writers Collaborative, 1978.

Goodson, Laurie and Betsy McLoughlin. *Altered Book Special Effects!* Fort Worth: Design Originals, 2003.

Greenfield, Jane. *ABC of Bookbinding*. New Castle: Oak Knoll Press, 1998.

Harrison, Holly. *Altered Books, Collaborative Journals, and Other Adventures in Bookmaking*. Gloucester: Rockport Publishers, 2003.

Johnson, Paul. *Literacy Through the Book Arts*. Portsmouth, NH: Heinemann, 1993.

Janeczko, Paul, editor. *The Place My Words Are Looking For*. NY: Bradley Press, 1990.

Koch, Kenneth. *Rose Where Did You Get That Red?* NY: Random House, 1973.

Koch, Kenneth and Kate Farrell. *Sleeping on the Wing: An Anthology of Modern Poetry with Essays on Reading and Writing*. NY: Vintage Books, 1982.

Koch, Kenneth. *Wishes, Lies, and Dreams*. New York: Harper & Row, 1970.

McMurtrie, Douglas C. The Book: *The Story of Printing & Bookmaking*. New York: Oxford University Press, 1957

Myers & Simms, *The Longman Dictionary of Poetic Terms*. NY: Longman Inc., 1989

Padgett, Ron, editor. *The Teachers & Writers Handbook of Poetic Forms*. New York: Teacher& Writers Collaborative, 1987.

Tsujimoto, Joseph I. *Teaching Poetry Writing to Adolescents*. Urbana, Illinois: National Council of Teachers of English, 1988.

Webberley, Marilyn and JoAn Forsyth. *Books, Boxes & Wraps: Binding & Building Step-by-Step*. Kirkland, WA: Bifocal Publishing, 1995.

13 Acknowledgements

Long in the works, *Building a Book, Binding a Poem* began as a chat between neighbors, grew as a collaboration between artists, developed into a friendship based on mutual respect and admiration, and finally has become a book. We first must acknowledge the priceless contributions of Jon Pastor, our publisher, designer, and Meg's husband, who believed in this project even when we'd tired of it or were distracted by "real work." And we both thank our husbands, Jon Pastor and Steve Morley, for their emotional and financial support of our various creative endeavors. We appreciate the careful reading and encouragement of Diane Anderson, and the interest of colleagues who swore they'd "use the book if only we'd finish writing it." We thank Christine Williams whose lovely and able hands are featured in the demo photographs. Finally, we are grateful to our students, past and present, whose feedback and creativity keeps it fresh.

www.ingramcontent.com/pod-product-compliance
Lightning Source LLC
LaVergne TN
LVHW061245100826
845148LV00008B/1035

* 9 7 8 0 9 7 9 5 8 6 1 0 1 *